Testimonials

Terry, I have read a lot of psychology text books and other "self-help" books, but after reading your book I believe it to be one of the best, possibly the best book I have read on overcoming depression, lethargy, feeling down, negative self-talk etc. It is concise, with no unnecessary jargon, and easy to comprehend. I think every high school student should be given a copy when they leave school – skills for life.
(With permission) Vivien Wornell, Social Worker/Counsellor, Veteran Liaison Officer, St. George Private Hospital

I have shared your books and the Stickman concepts with many people, including a very good friend of mine who has truly embraced Stickman following a relationship split. So much so, he now carries Stickman with him everywhere..... yes he has had Stickman tattooed, yes tattooed on his left arm, approx 6" tall......wow what a lady you are and you need to know you "make a difference"
(With permission) Stephen Lea, Director, Partner Alliance Development – Roman Catholic Archdiocese of Brisbane

I have provided a Mum with a copy as her son suicided some six months ago and she is struggling terribly (understandably). I also passed this book on to another Mum who is now bringing up her grandson due to a son (the father of this child) who suicided some three years. I gave her a Stickman and a copy of the children's book on health. She rang to say that this has turned this little one around and they spend a great deal of time discussing pit and stick. Terry, your books have helped … enormously and for that I am forever grateful.
(With permission) Marion McKay - Dip HRM, MBTI, Dip Counselling and Group Work

When you meet Terry in person or through this amazing book you immediately understand that her key values are integrity, generosity and insight. She incites her readers to examine the beliefs they employ to run their lives and with her encouragement to sack the, attitudes and habits that no longer serve them, making room to embrace ways of thinking and behaving that open the path to flourishing, joy and abundance. Terry truly practices what she preaches with zest. So don't stay asleep at the wheel of your life, wake up to purposeful living.
(With permission) Rev'd Nicholas Rundle, Workplace Chaplain/Coach, Master Practitioner of Neuro Semantic NLP, Mission Australia

The following are a few anonymous excerpts from letters received about "Two times in life …"

"Just before I moved here (Australia) I was given the book - There are two times in life - NOW & TOO LATE! and it has literally changed my life! I have adopted many of the catch phrases as a motivational tool to help me achieve the things that I want. It has been really exciting telling people about your book and even the title is one of those – 'shivers down your spine- lets get going' sentences!! I have just listened to your radio clip on the webpage and decided that you are sooo funny and now officially my number one idol …

Terry's book immediately helped me change my way of thinking and 'doing'. I have learnt such valuable lessons after reading it only once! I suffer from anxiety and depression . . . I know Terry's book would book would open a window to many, many people like me.

I bought her 'There are 2 times in life - Now & 2 late' Book. This book has become my bible and helped me so much.

My mother bought me a copy of Terry's book 'There are only two times in life...' This book totally inspired me; Stickman now lives beside my bed. I suffer from depression and the techniques in this book have helped me through a really tough period.

I borrowed a friend's copy of Terry's 'Now & Too Late' and have read it four times and would like my own copy. How can I get one?! I have suffered two strokes and rehabilitated myself very well using my own intuition and logic but occasionally I still succumb to the pit. 'Now & Too Late' struck a cord with me and I would like my own copy to help me on my journey of life having fun.

I have just finished reading your book titled 'There are two times in life....now & too late'. Can I say what an incredibly motivating and inspiring book- -many passages I kept reading over & over again. Such wisdom & insight! I have so many friends who would also benefit greatly from the information contained in this book.

I was very fortunate to win your book ... I started reading it ... and loved it! In places I laughed out loud and in others I just sobbed. Just really simple advice but so on the money!!

There are only two times in life

NOW &
TOO LATE!

Terry **Hawkins**

Illustrations by Mick Tate

First published in 2006

People In Progress Pty Ltd
PO Box 77, Palm Beach NSW 2108
www.peopleinprogress.com.au
www.terryhawkins.com.au

Hawkins, Terry L.
There are only two times in life now & too late!

ISBN 978-0-9775970-0-0.

1. Self-actualization (Psychology). I. Title.

158.1

Hawkins, Terry; Tarling, Lowell (ed); Tate, Mick (ill)
There are Two Times in Life... Now and Too Late

2nd edition ISBN 0-9775970-0-8

Editing: Lowell Tarling
Illustrations: Mick Tate
Printed by Griffin Press Australia
Project Management: Messenger Publishing

10 9 8 7 6 5 4

Acknowledgements

It's a strange and wonderful thing to write a book. I don't think I have ever been more confronted by myself. As you pound your way through the words, the range of emotions and reactions you experience is amazing.

This book would still be in my head, my heart and in my frustrations were it not for the countless "STICKMEN" I have met and heard of on my journey. To you I say the biggest thank you imaginable! Thank you for trusting me, thank you for your courage in letting STICKMAN rule and thank you for sharing a few words in our "book of life" together.

To Harison and Jackson, you are my little men and my brave giants. Your courage, insight and complete honesty are a constant reminder to me of why all of this matters. You keep me level and alive!

To Amber Shannon and the amazing People In Progress crew — WOW! It is difficult to find the words to acknowledge such powerful and supportive people. *People In Progress* is what it is because of you and I continue to grow and be all that I am meant to be because you believe in me. You truly are amazing. You were my courage when I was scared to start writing, you are also my dearest friends and colleagues.

To my beautiful mother! How can anyone write their first book and not acknowledge their mother. Mum you have left your footprints on my heart. I thank you and love you with all my soul. x

Table of contents

Introduction

For the last 25 years as a public speaker I have been given the privilege of working with hundreds of thousands of magnificent people.

This journey has led me to develop an insatiable fascination for the human spirit.

This book is a culmination of all the learnings that have had the greatest impact on my life. Stories of triumph, shock, inspiration and sadness have shaped me into the person I am today.

It was my desire to create an easy-to-read, user manual — a manual that could support you in getting and keeping your life on track.

A great deal of the content is scientific fact. For most of you though, this is unnecessary as your instinct will tell you if what I have written is true or not. Even if it sometimes hurts, our truth will always stir within us.

When this happens be still for a moment and pay attention. *Listen!*

So often we ignore the little signs that may guide us to wisdom.

It is this internal wisdom that knows what we need. It is this internal wisdom that teaches us how to move forward.

We all have to pay a price in life and the price we have to pay is we have to pay attention.

Enjoy!

~Terry~

Until one is committed there is hesitancy,
the chance to draw back, always ineffectiveness.

Concerning all acts of initiative (and creation)
there is one elementary truth, the ignorance of
which kills countless ideas and splendid plans:

That the moment one definitely commits oneself
then Providence moves too. All sorts of things
occur to help one that would never otherwise
have occurred.

A whole stream of events arise from the
decision raising in one's favour, all manner of
unforeseen incidents and meetings and material
assistance which no one could have dreamt
would come their way.

Whatever you can do or dream you can, begin it.
Boldness has genius, power and magic in it.

Begin it now!

A passage from Johann Wolfgang von Goethe
(1749–1832) German poet, dramatist, politician and
philosopher.

Chapter **1**

There are only two times in life... now & too late

Life is what happens to you when you're busy making other plans.

Beautiful Boy, John Lennon

There are only two times in life… now & too late!

O ne afternoon while sitting in my office, I began reading over the participant list for our next management program to be held in Perth. While scrolling the names I noticed a hand-written note beside one of the names of a participant. It said 'husband died four weeks previous'. I gasped, it was Lynn! She had participated in our C.A.R.E (Customers are Really Everything®) program just over one year ago.

They say that laughter is the best medicine and I later learned that Lynn had requested to be a part of our next course because she was in so much distress that she needed to learn to laugh again. And so the course began and we started introducing ourselves to each other. Eventually it was Lynn's turn to speak, and after I asked her how she was feeling, she replied "Not that good!"

I thoughtlessly said "Oh, why not? It can't be that bad!" Her face reddened, her eyes filled with tears and in that moment I remembered the note. It was *her* husband who had died four weeks earlier. I didn't know what to say. I couldn't imagine what it was like to experience that kind of loss.

I felt so stupid and awkward for being flippant yet despite my *faux pas* her warmth and love covered my discomfort, which is when she said that she had come to the program because she wanted to laugh again. Her recent life had been so sad and she was happy to be here. I remember the sadness and helplessness I felt in that moment.

Well, that night when I went to bed in my hotel room, I let my imagination run without boundaries. I tried to imagine what it would be like to lose someone that close to me — someone who I loved with all my heart. I imagined myself never having that person in my life again. It hurt.

The pain stretched through every limb, every vein, and every heartbeat.

It was almost too much for me to bear, yet here before me was a woman who had the courage to confront her deepest anguish, face the world and allow herself to laugh and cry as she needed without burdening anyone with her grief.

Behind every face lies an amazing story! This is something I am reminded of every day. Whenever you look at a stranger's face, I wonder what story they could tell you?

Lynn spent the next couple of days immersing herself in the program. I recall one particular section of the program where Lynn actually laughed so much, she cried.

As she wiped away the tears she told us how wonderful it was to be crying from happiness not sadness.

It is hard to find the words to describe how special that moment was. It will be etched in the memories of all of us who sat in the room that day.

When Lynn talked about her husband, her entire face lit up. He was her soul-mate, her lover, her everything! After many years in a previous unhappy marriage, this wonderful man gave her the joy that had previously eluded her.

They were building their dream home and to speed things along financially he moved from his position at the Customs

3

Department (where he had been for 20 years) to take up a courier's position.

Six weeks later he walked into a building, took a breath at the wrong time and contracted Legionnaire's Disease. Ten days later he was dead!

He was her mate, her lover, her confidante and friend, now he was gone.

I was still speechless and in shock when she handed me a piece of paper, a prose called "The Present".

"This was his favourite!" she said. I don't think I have ever read more meaningful or sage advice on how to live. (I have included a copy of this prose at the end of this book)

In that moment I looked at the sadness in her eyes and I felt an urgent need to take her emptiness away. I wanted her to be happy which is when I realised that I was responding to my own fears of losing those that I loved.

Grief is a necessary part of healing. By wanting Lynn to not feel this I was somehow protecting myself from the pain of death. We try so hard to run away from the really painful emotions of life yet they must be experienced otherwise we can't move on.

Over the next 12 months I saw Lynn a few times at my presentations and workshops. We also sent each other occasional emails, including one about a monkey where she laughed so much she got a stitch!!!

In one of these emails she asked me to make a tape recording for her. She said she needed something that spoke to her, and her alone, to get her through the dark days.

She said "Terry, you say things that inspire me and make me feel alive. Get me out of this rut I'm in, make me a tape that I can play in the car when I'm feeling down."

I promised her I would send it.

The next time I saw 'beautiful' Lynn was November 2000 at a one-day workshop I was conducting in Perth.

She asked about the tape and I apologised for not sending it. I confessed that I was so nervous about what she may have thought that I didn't get around to doing it because I didn't want to embarrass myself.

She reassured me, encouraged me, and even begged me to do it. We had a few laughs, a big hug and… I promised her I would do it by Christmas.

Well, time rolled by and I thought about that tape nearly everyday.

I kept thinking about how special Lynn was and how pathetic I was for procrastinating on the tape. The truth was I was nervous of what others might think about what I would say.

I kept asking myself "What was I waiting for?" Did I need my message to be perfect? Should it be profound? And who was I to judge that anyway?

I was paralysed with indecision just thinking about it!

Then came the New Year and the phone rang.

The conversation went like this, "Do you know Lynn from Perth?"

"Why, yes!" I said with a touch of guilt, remembering the unfinished tape.

"She died last night in her sleep!"

There are only two times in life… now & too late!

There are only two times in life… now & too late!

I preach that phrase. I say it practically every day of my life and for the most part I live it because there really *are* only two times in life — this moment and then it's gone!

We all get afraid at times but it is so sad when that fear completely paralyses us from moving forward. This is not a message about physical death. It is a message about the death we have while we are still alive. I'd rather be alive than one of the "living dead!"

I cried for Lynn, I cried for me. I cried that I didn't do what she thought I was capable of doing. I cried for the fact that I could have made her life a little easier — but I didn't. Why?

…because I was afraid!

Life is full of learning experiences. It is packed with situations that give us wisdom and understanding but what if those experiences are so hurtful that we get stuck in the pain and stop moving forward?

Not more than 24 hours had passed when I received another phone call. A young man I had worked with a few weeks before; a beautiful, talented, intelligent 21-year old man had been sentenced to prison for a drug offence. It was like being hit by a second bullet.

Again there was sadness in my heart.

Remembering his beautiful innocent face, I think of him now, a young man with a promising future. I just find it hard to accept him being locked away with hardened criminals in a maximum security prison cell.

The trifecta came a few days later. A friend called to tell me his 18-year old sister had tried to kill herself. She had jumped off a four storey bridge and survived! How desperate she must have been to not see a way out and make an attempt on her own life? (She was clearly meant to live.)

I wanted to scream and yell for all three of them! I've heard thousands of stories from people who have been to Hell and back. After training and presenting to thousands of people, I began drawing some conclusions, which lead me to write this book.

The biggest conclusion I have made (and I know I'm right on this one) is that I have yet to meet anyone who has had a charmed life.

Every person that I have ever met has experienced something in their past, from which they still carry scars, some of which are more painful than others.

Some of the scars are self-inflicted, others are not. The most painful memories are usually emphasised as a result of us wanting to numb the feeling by running away from something.

A young man with his whole future in front of him, now

in prison; a teenager so desperate to silence her pain, now confronts her own survival. What controls their destiny?

How will these experiences affect their lives?

Is the actual experience the defining moment in their lives?

NO!

How they perceive these experiences will define how they will live the rest of their lives. **That** will be their defining moment.

The pain associated with avoiding something hurtful is usually far greater than the pain of confrontation.

Yet most of us spend our life running away or trying to avoid the pain of these scars.

We all have a story. Something from our past that shakes our centre and puts a spin on how we see the world.

We cannot change what has happened to us. We only have the power to change our perception and response to these events.

It is neither the incidents nor the people in our lives that damage us, it is the meaning we place on these external influences.

Your past does not hurt you!

What hurts is the meaning you ascribe to it. Change its meaning and you will change the feelings you have about past experiences because when you change your perceptions your brain responds to those changes biologically. FACT!

**Two men in jail,
looking through the bars,
one sees mud,
the other sees the stars.**

Think about a difficult situation in your past. Every time you recall that memory do you experience a negative emotion? Is it grief? Embarrassment? Shame? Guilt? Betrayal? Disgust? Dismay? Fear? Sadness?

Of course in the initial stages of an experience or during the grieving or healing process certain emotions are vital, but why is it when we recall particular incidents years, sometimes decades later, we still have the same intensity of feeling as we felt at the time it happened?

We can get so locked in the emotion of an incident that we spend our lifetime replaying the event. We don't move on. We just keep playing the tape over and over in our heads and every time we play it we feel the same painful feelings.

This is usually because we are in an associated state. An 'associated state' is where we imagine ourselves to be in the actual experience. And when we recreate these same feelings it is because we have remembered the situation whilst in a fully associated state. We see it through our own eyes and relive it as if we are actually there in the present.

What if you were to change the way you perceived a painful situation from your past?

When you are dissociated you no longer have the emotional attachment therefore the feeling disappears or dissipates. Imagine you're looking at yourself on a movie screen and this event is playing out before your eyes. You are watching yourself and yet you feel detached (or dissociated).

As you watch the imagined screen, ask yourself, "What did I learn from this experience?" If you were to tell the person on the screen (you) what was gained from this experience as an objective observer, what would you say? What did you learn as a result of this experience?

Compassion? Forgiveness? Courage? Insight? Patience? Respect? Integrity? Humility? Sensitivity? Understanding? Love? Surrender? Did you learn the right way to handle the problem? Did you gain empathy for yourself and others in the same situation?

Visualise the place in your past that offers you the learning from that painful experience.

Evaluate how that experience has shaped you and you will surely see that, regardless of the pain, this experience has provided you with a depth of wisdom and understanding. Furthermore, as you reassess its meaning you will notice your feelings about the event will also change.

Even though we still may be affected by these situations we no longer allow our emotions to paralyse and restrain us from moving forward.

I remember watching a war movie and I recall a scene where immediately before going into battle, a soldier confessed to his superior, "I don't think I should be telling you this but I'm terrified".

His boss wisely replied, "Oh did they forget to tell you in training school? *Courage only comes after you have faced the fear.*"

Even though he was wracked with fear, that soldier still went into battle. He managed his fear and didn't allow his emotions to immobilise or paralyse him.

A very gentle, softly spoken woman came up to me during

a training session and told me how her son had been sexually abused at the age of nine (he is now an adult).

My heart ached for her and for her baby. She then told me her greatest personal pain was that she too had also been abused as a child and not even this awareness helped her protect her child. Her greatest anguish came from failing to safeguard the most precious part of her child's life, his innocence. She went on to tell me, that although they experienced much pain and sadness together, they also shared a feeling of freedom and bonding. Her son's honesty allowed her to share with him her "dark" past (as she put it). This opening up of truth allowed mother and son to begin their healing process together.

One of my personal examples is that I too experienced sexual abuse as a child.

Note that I chose the word "experienced" rather than "survived" or "suffered". In expressing past anxieties many people use dramatic languaging that keeps them in a negative state. How does that saying go? "I'm not surviving, I'm thriving, thanks very much."

For many years I allowed myself to feel shattered by this incident along with many other "learning experiences" that life thrust upon me. Each time I revisited the memory I clung to the pain it had brought me.

But it wasn't the physical aspect that affected me most, it was the betrayal of trust.

I have two beautiful sons Harison 12 and Jackson 9. Shortly before Harison's birth, I heard someone speaking about how changing the meaning of a situation will change our feelings about it.

At first I was angry to hear such dismissive words.

How could anyone speak so flippantly and suggest that I could change how I felt about a situation simply by changing the way I thought about it?

Did they know the pain I had endured? Did they know the repercussions of such an event?

Something was stinging inside (the truth!) so I knew some issue had "come up" for me. It was time to "PAY ATTENTION". It was time to really LISTEN.

As those words rang in my ears, I decided to ponder this new concept.

"What if I changed the meaning I had placed on the sexual abuse?"

"What if I were to look at it differently and detach myself from my usual highly charged reaction?

I thought about my new baby, I thought about what advice I would have given to that little girl who was me all those years ago?

Sometimes we get so stuck in the pain of the memory, we don't see the magnificent learning and wisdom that is available to us.

I thought about how I could change this painful memory into a powerful learning experience.

I forced myself to give up the anger and resentment so I could find the learning.

What did I learn?

I learned that I had an opportunity to teach my children how to protect their bodies.

I learned something that would have helped me, which is that little people need an automatic response if they are ever placed in a potentially dangerous situation.

It's ridiculous to say to kids, *"Don't talk to strangers"*, because we make them talk to strangers everyday ("Say hello to Mrs Smith...").

And "Don't accept a lift from someone you don't know" isn't totally foolproof advice because perpetrators are very clever at tricking children into trusting them.

We have to give our children responses that are drilled into them so that they are not powerless should they ever find themselves in such situations. (That would have helped me.)

No one told me that it was okay to stand up to people who were going to do "bad" things to me. I didn't even know they were bad at first, I was so young.

In a defining moment many years later, I changed the meaning I placed on my sexual abuse experience. I changed my outlook from "victim" to "empowerment".

That experience gave me the insight into how to teach my children to protect themselves.

God forbid anything like that might ever happen to them, but at least I am in a position where I can tell them what to say and do if they are ever placed in that unfortunate situation.

My children are drilled every week, "If someone tries to touch you or your penis, what do you say and do?"

In a really loud, strong voice they are told to yell, "NO! GO AWAY, I DON'T KNOW YOU!"

And then they know to run to me or another woman and tell them what transpired. (Only a very small percentage of women are perpetrators.)

It needs to become a default mechanism — an instant response. By age 3½ both my boys could say their name, address, phone number and their doctor's name.

They would recite it over and over. It's amazing how many five year olds don't even know their phone number.

I'm passionate about teaching kids how to protect themselves. I'm passionate about people leaving the pain of their past behind.

I am passionate about all of us living the life we were meant to live.

My version of Hell is getting to the end of your life and someone saying, "*This* is the life you were *supposed* to live! *This* is what you could have done had you not been so afraid!"

By changing the meaning we place on situations we can start to see a way out. If you are finding it hard to change the meaning of an experience, interact with someone who has experienced a similar problem.

We start healing ourselves by healing others.

We all have a lot to share. For example, if you experienced sexual abuse, become a volunteer for a children's sexual abuse ward at a hospital.

If you were physically, mentally or intellectually abused, go work with disadvantaged youth.

15

If you hated the poverty of your past, serve at a soup kitchen one day a month.

If you hated your parents working, go to work in an orphanage.

When we step outside of the "picture" of our own past and see first hand someone playing the cards they were dealt in a positive way, we begin to understand that our own past wasn't as bad as we imagined.

I recall a conversation with a participant in one of my programs many years ago, a compassionate young woman with whom I had worked a year or so before. Little did I realise that throughout the first program she held a very shocking secret. Her conversation went something like this.

"Terry, I have really gained a lot from doing volunteer work. It has helped me to get over the pain of what happened to me."

"What happened to you?" I asked with curiosity.

"Two years ago I was abducted by a group of guys, kept in the boot of their car and continuously raped for a week!"

I still get a chill when I recall that conversation.

I don't think many of us could even comprehend such a terrifying experience, let alone move on with our life to help those less fortunate.

However, there is an amazing saying, "We see so far because we can stand on the shoulders of giants."

By overcoming her past this wonderful girl is a giant for us all.

She didn't allow the trauma of this horrid experience to paralyse her.

She grieved, she ached, she cried for a long time, she did lots of healing and then she moved to a place in her soul that could help her to ease other people's pain.

Is this hard to believe? I can hear some of you saying, "It can't be that easy?"

I recall someone in a training session sharing the same view.

"It's not that easy to let go!" she remarked quite angrily and another participant replied, "Well you must be hanging on too tight!"

How's that for wisdom!

We see so far because we can stand on the shoulders of giants.

There are two times in life…
now & too late!

Courage only
comes after you
have faced
the fear.

We start healing
ourselves by
healing others.

Chapter **2**

Knowing why isn't enough!

Film director and actor, Woody Allen, is quoted as saying "I've spent 30 years in therapy and I can tell you every disorder I have and why. I just don't know *how* to change them!"

Finding the wisdom from our pain and then *doing* something about it are two very different things.

I meet a lot of people who are completely into discovering the 'why' of their past but unfortunately that's where they stop.

"Why did we move 17 times in 17 years?" "Why do I attract men who abuse me?" "Why do I drink so much?" "Why am I so obsessed with winning?" "Why am I so insecure?"

We discover the 'why' and yet fail to *do* anything with it. We fail to continue the journey into the really challenging arena of changing the way we *do* our lives.

We know *why* we are the way we are yet we continue to replicate the same pattern of negativity.

The only way for us to live a different life is not only to learn from what we have experienced but more importantly to take action in order to get a different result in the future.

Let me give you an example. Let's say in their younger years, some people felt insecure around their parents because their parents were way too critical of them — perhaps cruelly. Yet even when (later in life) these people become empowered, they *still* do nothing when their parents continue to hassle them in the same way. Why? Because they fear the confrontation.

They fail to take affirmative action because confrontation would be too uncomfortable. Well, 'nothing changes if nothing changes'.

One of the most important influencers of change is our awareness of our communication with others as well as our personal communication (or internal dialogue).

Imagine this scenario: an aggressive guy walks up to the check-in counter at an international airport. In a loud, gruff voice he says to the attendant, "Jack Byrne — Toronto!" and throws his passport on the counter, indifferent to the fact that he struck the attendant's hand in the process.

As the attendant checks the screen, she cringes. Mr Byrne's flight closed 15 minutes ago and she isn't looking forward to delivering the bad news. She looks up at Mr Byrne who is impatiently tapping his fingers on the counter and says in a most apologetic voice, "I am so sorry sir, that flight is now closed and unfortunately......"

Not letting her complete her sentence, he bursts into a tirade of abuse.

"What do you mean the flight is closed? Re-open it! Call the plane immediately. Let them know I've arrived!"

The attendant tries to pacify Mr Byrne. "Sir, I can imagine your frustration. It's just that...", but she is again interrupted by another blast.

"Don't give me that! Do you know who I am! Who do you think you are you blonde bimbo! I'm going to have your job for this, just you wait!"

He storms off leaving the attendant standing there to receive her next customer in an unruffled way. "Good afternoon, sir," she says in a calm and professional manner. "Thank you for your patience."

The next customer cannot believe the attendant's amazing ability to handle such a horrid outburst and then instantly switch her headspace to being emotionally ready to receive the next customer.

"I just have to say that I have never seen anyone handle such an aggressive person in such a calm and empathic way. You are amazing! How do you do it?"

"Welllllll", she says with a cheeky smile appearing on her face, "I have a secret way of dealing with people like that..."

"Oh, do tell?" the customer replied.

"All I can say is that I would love to be in Toronto to see Mr Byrnes' face when he finds out that his luggage has gone to Tokyo!"

As they both burst out laughing, the flight attendant admitted that she was only kidding, "But it is an enticing thought," she quipped. "We all have bad days and although I was a little shaken by his rudeness, I accept it wasn't really about me. Maybe he doesn't know how to handle situations like that or maybe he's had a bad day."

This attendant is a perfect example of how powerful changing our perception can be.

She didn't react emotionally to Mr Byrnes' tirade. Instead she stepped outside of the situation and was able to put herself in his shoes.

The attendant could handle him because instead of becoming associated with the situation she was dissociated.

This book is about helping us to turn ugly, painful, hurtful situations and memories into tools and catalysts that can centre us in the present and propel us into a powerful and free future.

It's about taking action regardless of how we feel.

It's about moving forward so we don't allow the people, places and perceptions that have hurt us in our past, limit the possibility of us creating a powerful future.

Take action,
regardless of
how you feel.

Chapter **3**

It's not always about you

We often confuse empathy with sympathy. Empathy is having the ability to put yourself into someone else's shoes and see things as they do.

It is about being able to understand another person's thoughts, feelings and opinions without becoming emotionally involved. Empathy refrains from passing judgement and avoids categorising a person as being right or wrong.

I'm sure you're probably the most empathic person you know!!! So let's put your empathy gene to the test, shall we? There you are, driving in the traffic, enjoying yourself, maybe even grooving to your favourite tune when all of a sudden another car comes out of nowhere and cuts you off!

You slam on the brakes, you swerve to avoid a collision, the whole thing feels like a near death experience and as you push your heart back down your throat, you wind down your window and say in a calm warm voice, "I totally understand your situation. You probably didn't see me."

YEAH RIGHT!!!

What are fingers for if not to abuse other drivers?

I'm sure the majority of us would see ourselves as caring, loving, enthusiastic, passionate and kind people. However *being* those traits is a completely different thing.

Let's try another situation. You arrive home in the evening to greet your partner. You've had a great day and in you walk. "Hi honey, I'm home!" you say in your cheeriest voice.

In the distance you hear nothing more than a miserable grunt. "Oh darling," you respond. "You don't seem to be your normal happy self. What's up sugar plum?"

AS IF! It probably goes more like,

You:	"Hi honey!"
Partner:	(grunt)
You:	"Don't snap at me!"
Partner:	"I didn't, a grunt is not a snap".
You:	"Don't be pedantic, what's wrong with you!!!'
Partner:	"Just because I'm not all over you doesn't mean there is anything wrong!!!".
You:	"Who do you think you are!"

And before you know it, it is on for young and old.

Sometimes we think we are being empathic when we are actually falling into an automatic sympathetic state.

Many of us confuse empathy with sympathy. Being sympathetic means we take on the feelings and behaviours of the other person. Sympathy is when we pity ourselves or someone else.

We feel sorry for them or we buy into their sadness, hurt, anger, frustration, pain, etc, after which we mirror this behaviour. It goes like this, they're angry, so we become angry. They're sad, so we get sad. They're frustrated, so we switch to frustration. They're cranky, so we get cranky too.

Have you had a friend, spouse, lover or family member talk to you about a situation after which you have gone straight into feeling what they feel?

For example they may tell you of a situation at work where someone has been "picking" on them.

We usually go straight into defending our loved one and condemning the work colleague. We may think we're comforting them but we are actually offering a false sense of comfort.

If anything, sympathy can make the person feel more frightened, lonely and worse. We say, "Oh you poor thing, I feel so sorry for you".

Sympathy can also be a self-centred reaction because our response is about how *we* would feel if something like that happened to us.

In contrast, empathy is not about us — it is completely about the other person. When we have true empathy we don't cloud the situation with our feelings, thoughts and opinions.

We use our imaginative skills to picture what it must be like for *the other person* to experience this situation.

The great thing about being empathic is it also stops us

from 'assuming' which gives us the chance to ask inquiring questions.

So often we interpret situations on the basis of our own beliefs, values, and experiences — only to find out that we are completely out of sync with how the other person *really* feels.

I recall a lovely man whom I met after a conference. He mentioned how he was having trouble connecting with his 15-year old daughter and said they seemed to be growing apart.

She rarely spent time with him, unlike his older daughter who seemed to enjoy the same things he did.

This father really wanted to work on their relationship but everything he tried to do seemed to push his daughter away even more.

He seemed upset by this and as he spoke, I could see tears in his eyes. I asked him if he had honestly told his daughter how he was *feeling* and how much he loved her and that he wanted to get closer to her, rather than just over-analysing why they weren't connecting.

They had never discussed these matters and he resolved to do so at his soonest opportunity.

I received an email from him a few days later saying that he sat his daughter down and simply told her how he was feeling.

He told her he didn't have any answers. He just wanted her to know how much he wanted to be closer to her and that he loved her with all his heart. He told her the beautiful, blatant truth about *himself* not what he expected from her or their relationship.

Once he opened up and showed his vulnerability, his daughter was immediately empathic. They cried, hugged and agreed to spend more time getting to know each other.

This father and daughter proceeded on a wonderful journey of creating a great relationship based on understanding and love, not judgment and false expectations.

How strange that we can spend so much time living together without putting in the time to *understand* each other. The reason for this is usually because we're too busy and as a consequence, we find ourselves wanting everyone else to understand *us* so that our needs get filled first.

One of the keys to a successful relationship is to remember that whatever we want for ourselves we must also be willing to give.

Empathy is completely about the other person.

Chapter **4**

How to have a great relationship

I have the formula for a happy, fulfilling relationship. Yes I do!

Just because I am a divorced, single mum you might be thinking that this will be like getting advice on how to cook a steak from a vegetarian!!

But I've been around the block a few times and I *do* know the formula, it's just that it takes two to make it work.

Are you ready for this ground breaking news?

Here it is...

Find out what the other person wants and give it to them.

When was the last time you asked someone you love, "How do you know I love you?"

And what if someone asked the same of you?

We can usually articulate what makes us feel loved.

So let's just say that I ask Harison, "How do you know Mummy loves you?" and he answers, "Because you sit with me while I play on the computer." Then, what if I was to say, "I don't really enjoy that, pick something else"? How would he feel?

Or...let's say you're a manager and you ask a team member, "What motivates you?" and they say "I am motivated when you spend 30 minutes with me each week". What if you then say, "I don't really have time for that, what else motivates you? How about I give you a bonus instead?"

Mmmm, makes us think, doesn't it? I'm sure most of you will agree that we only give people what makes them happy if it fits with what *we* want to give them.

Find out what the other person wants and give it to them. It sounds simple in theory, but in practice it may not be what we want to do.

But if we truly love someone and want them to be happy then we will willingly give them what they want (without compromising our own values and beliefs).

I recall a woman approaching me at a conference after I had just discussed this concept. Her face lit up as she told me she was getting married in four months time. She mentioned she loved receiving flowers and as her smile faded she continued.

"But my fiancée won't buy me any?" almost searching for

a reason. Puzzled, I asked "Why not?" "He said he doesn't *'do'* flowers". Came the disappointed reply.

"Well!" I began, "Why don't you tell him that 'the shop is shut!' and it's not opening for business until we see some petals sitting in a vase!!! It's called 'consequence' baby!" We both laughed and then in a very serious tone I added the punch-line, "You're not even married yet and if he isn't willing to buy you a lousy bunch of flowers every now and then to put a smile on your face, what else is he not going to be willing to do to make you happy after you're married?"

I don't know whether she was angry or saddened but there in her face, I could see my words rang true.

Once we get used to our partners, we tend to stop doing the magical things that we used to do for each other. We don't bother with surprise gifts, a lingering kiss before leaving for work, cooking their favourite meals and more.

After they're married, men tend to complain about insufficient sex in their relationships. Before marriage it was all about chocolates, dinners, walks along the beach and whispering sweet nothings. After marriage, "hey babe, are you awake?" Someone even came up with the Jelly Bean Theory. You know the one? If you put a jelly bean in the jar each time you have sex before marriage and then take one out for every time you have sex after you are married, you will never empty the jar!

Well guys, we girls have our own jelly bean jar too.

I often say to men, if you kept doing what you did at the beginning of the relationship, then we women would have kept doing what we did at the beginning of the relationship — think about it!

A group of procrastinators attended one of my management programs and I set them a task for homework.

"When you get home tonight, do one thing that you've been putting off. We'll report back to base tomorrow."

On the way home in the car I mentioned to my then husband Rick that I was going to cook him his favourite meal, which is something I had been putting off for a while.

"I'm making you Spaghetti Bolognaise tonight honey!" I said so proudly, knowing just how much he adored it.

He paused for a moment... "Ah, honey it's not Bol-OG-naise! It's bolognaise, the G is silent!"

"Really!" I exclaimed, "and is that like Rick with a silent P!!! I't's okay, he laughed too!"

Sometimes we miss the magic in the intention because we are looking for fault in the person.

34

Most of the time the things that make people feel loved are not hard to give.

I love it when you empty the dishwasher.
I love it when you take me for a meal so we can sit and talk, and be together, alone.
I love it when you pick some flowers for me.
I love it when you give me a surprise massage.
I love it when you clean up the dishes after dinner.
I love it when you make dinner.
I love it when you help me in the garden.
When I say I need time to think, I love it when you let me be alone.
I love it when you help me with my homework.
I love it when you surprise me at work and drive me home.
I love it when you send me an "I love you" message.
I love it when you tell me "I love you".
I love it when you brush my hair.
I love it when we have fish and chips at the beach.
I love how you want to get to know my friends.
I love it when you tell me I look gorgeous even though you've seen this same face for 20 years.
I love it how you still laugh at my jokes even though you've heard them a thousand times before.
I love how you're willing to do whatever it takes to make me happy.

Here's an exercise for you:

List 10 positive traits that you love about your partner, parent, child or work buddy, someone you really care about. Remember no but's or however's...

Write down those 10 things about them and then...

...just give it to them.

Find out what the other person wants and give it to them.

If you're a vegetarian, learn how to cook steak.

Sometimes
we miss the
magic in the
intention because
we are looking
for fault in
the person.

Chapter **5**

Get out of that PIT!

Have you ever been in a mindset where you have decided to get fit?

You know the feeling; you feel it's time to turn your life around from being a lazy loafer to a lean, mean healthy machine.

You start the week like the reincarnation of Olympian Jesse Owens. You set the alarm for 5.30am. The moment it goes off you spring out of bed and you change into your exercise clothes.

Off you go, with a bounce in your step and a vision of being the next marathon winner at the Olympic Games.

You get on the running machine and push up that hill. You hop on the weights and complete three sets on each.

The sweat is dripping from you like Niagara Falls — aahhh, what a workout!

Day Two. (It's probably safe to say it's a Tuesday) and Beep! Beep! Beep!

The alarm goes off. This time you have a little conversation with yourself.

"I'm really tired this morning and I've got a huge day at work ahead of me. My legs are so sore from yesterday's workout. I really think I should take it a bit easy. I could do myself some serious harm if I overdo it. I could sleep in and go to the gym after work. My muscles won't be as sore by then. Yeah! I'll have a sleep in, I deserve it! Ahh! SNOOZE!"

Have you ever been in this headspace? We usually go there when we want to implement change in our life whether for exercise, eating, completing assignments or work projects or even when we vow to be more patient with our kids...it's that crucial moment when we decide to take a certain path.

So what's the key factor between staying in bed and getting up to go for that run?

The answer is PITMAN and STICKMAN!

You know the difference between positive and negative thinking? It is the perception of a glass being half full or half empty.

Now before you start saying that you've heard this all before, let me assure you that this book will provide you with the essential tools to identify what causes negative and positive behaviour. If you read on I will teach you how to overcome negativities through the power of Mind Language®.

I have turned these two states of behaviour into two characters that we can easily identify with — PITMAN and STICKMAN!

(I use the male gender only in reference to 'hu-man')

These two characters live inside your head. The villain (PITMAN) represents your negative state. The Superhero (STICKMAN) creates and reinforces your positive state.

They are the lead characters in the internal movie that we play every day in the movie theatre inside our head. This film enacts our moment-by-moment perceptions of events and situations that occur in our day.

40

The plot of this internal movie is the story of your life as it unfolds.

Let's first get a really clear picture of who PITMAN is, so that you can instantly recognise him when he wants to play havoc with your life.

Where does PITMAN live?

The PIT, of course!

But he doesn't just live in any old PIT, he lives in the PIT of Misery!

We've all been to the PIT haven't we? We all have experiences when life gets a little too hard and we feel downcast.

You know the PIT? It's the place we go to when life seems wretched, lonely, when we feel beaten, when everyone is against us and when no one understands us.

We visit the PIT when we think we haven't got enough money, or when we think we're too fat, too lonely, too tired, too lost or just fed up! We go there when we think we're being picked on, left behind, being criticised or pushed too far. Consequently we can feel angry, mean, helpless, nasty, afraid, PITiful — like a victim.

It's where we feel sorry for ourselves when life gets a little too hard.

When you are in the PIT of Misery you are a living, breathing, walking, talking PITMAN!

Some of us go to the PIT for an hour, others go there for a day, and there are many of us who go to the PIT a bit too often. Some people live their entire life in the PIT. We all go to the PIT. It's how long we stay there that makes all the difference.

When I was young and single, we used to enjoy the "doona dive" days — the days when we'd dive into bed, pull the doona over our head and hope the rest of the world would go away.

The easiest way to describe PIT Behaviour is to say that it is any behaviour that has a negative effect on ourselves or those around us.

Warning: If you have just told yourself, "Yeah, but you don't know how bad my life is...!"

That is serious PIT talk.

This book is about helping you to identify when you are in PIT danger and how to build yourself a ladder so that you can get out of the PIT.

A lot of us don't recognise when we are in the PIT but there are many telltale signs of PIT behaviour and being able to recognise them is half the journey.

PIT POSTURE

When we're being a PIT person, we take on PIT posture. We walk with our head and shoulders down, with our eyes and mouth also downcast.

When we're in the PIT we adopt a defeated POSTURE. We tend to walk slowly, dragging our feet behind us. We feel heavy, as if the weight of the world is on our shoulders.

PIT posture is not isolated to this sluggish manner. PIT PEOPLE sometimes have aggressive body language.

They sometimes throw their hands in the air, roll their eyes, and give looks that could decalcify a spine at 600 yards!

You can see a PIT PERSON coming from afar. You're feeling great, feeling happy, feeling good until you see the PIT PERSON ready to engage in a conversation you would rather avoid.

You hope he or she goes the other way but that doesn't happen. So in your cheeriest voice you ask the question you should never ask if you don't want it answered, "Hi, how are you today?" The shoulders droop further followed by the reply, "Oh, don't even ask!"

And you can feel your energy being sucked right out of you. "What's wrong with this person?" you ask yourself.

The answer is that the PITMAN State is his or her habitual way of life. People can actually get used to feeling flat. They get used to having a slouched posture (to the extent where the muscles actually modify into a hunched posture, which in turn affects their general sense of wellbeing).

Eventually they get so used to looking for the downside that they cease to notice the fabulous things that are occurring around them.

Don't let this happen to you.

PIT PRATTLE

Now PIT PEOPLE with their PIT POSTURE also have PIT PRATTLE! We all have a little voice inside of our head that chats away. If you've just asked yourself 'What voice?" That's it! Introduce yourself! PIT PEOPLE have all of this PIT PRATTLE going on inside their heads a lot of the time.

We all go to the PIT from time to time. The important difference is how long we spend there. PITMAN can turn up anywhere, anytime, if we let him.

When we're in the PIT, this little voice will chat away in a negative and defeatist way.

"I hate my life."

"How could any one love me?"

"I'll never be any good."

"I'm so hopeless."

"I'll never get over this hang-up."

"I'll be lonely all my life."

"I hate my job."

"Why did they do this to me?"

"How will I ever cope?"

"I'll never get any better."

"I need more money."

"I can't stand this anymore."

"I'm sick."

"I'll never get out of this Hell-hole."

"I can't change, I've been this way all my life."

"I'm stuck in this job, relationship, town...blah, blah, blah."

Did you know that optimism alters the nervous system and boosts the immune response while negativity depresses it?

PIT PRATTLE is incredibly pessimistic and PIT PEOPLE tend to criticise themselves and others harshly.

They complain constantly about their partners, their jobs, their lives, their kids, the traffic, the weather, TV commercials, the price of food, today's youth, today's elderly, last night's dinner and tomorrow's dessert!! They only see what *isn't* happening in their lives.

It's as if they can't control themselves, it's never their own fault, the fault always lies elsewhere. And if you even attempt to offer a more positive outlook, they will give you countless reasons why you're wrong.

You have to be very careful when hanging out with people who have made their PIT too cozy because helping someone who spends a lot of time in the PIT can be very seductive. This is known as the Rescuer Syndrome.

You may at first think that *you* are that special someone that can turn this person's life around. You may think your wisdom, your advice and your guidance will change him or her. So many people desperately want to help someone they love who has become comfortable in their PIT. They want to help so much that they join them.

No one can help a PIT DWELLER who doesn't *want* to be helped. Sure we can encourage, guide and support, but no one can get us out of the PIT when we're in it and we can't get anyone else out either.

It's our personal responsibility to pay attention when PITMAN is lurking around, trying to entice us back into that PIT.

Some time ago I made a habit of going to the gym every morning which I had been doing for about five weeks. This particular morning I woke up at 5.45am feeling tired and sore.

Well, there he was — PITMAN — with his little face at my window, whispering in a windy voice,

"It's cold out here — stay in bed where you're cozy and warm". It took all my might to ignore him.

Have you ever been on a health kick? You announce your resolutions then you open the pantry door and there he is again — PITMAN, sitting on the top shelf calling, "The chockie biscuits are up here!"

PITMAN accompanies you when you decide to have a few drinks with your friends after work. Precisely when you decide you'll be sensible, stop drinking and go home he says, "Go on, one more won't hurt!" He also adds the advice — "Just drink lots of water, you'll be fine in the morning".

PITMAN is everywhere.

Watch yourself.

We all go to
the PIT.

The important
decision is
how long you
choose to
stay there!

Chapter **6**

PIT language

*P*ay attention to your languaging. Be aware of the different phrases that are used by people when they're in the PIT. Avoid using such expressions yourself, or if you do, take that as an indication to turn yourself around:

- Can you believe how disgustingly hot it is?
- Rain always depresses me
- I'm nothing without him/her
- I've never been any good at…
- My kids are so annoying
- I've never got time for myself
- I find it impossible to make friends
- I wish she/he would grow up
- I can't believe I was so stupid!
- It's alright for you, you don't know…
- Why are they doing this to me?
- Why is this happening to me?
- What did I do to deserve this?

- I wish I had more money
- I wish I had less...
- I wish I didn't have so much work
- I wish I had a new job
- I wish these people would leave me alone
- I wish I wasn't alone
- I hate this town

For most of us PITMAN is just an occasional visitor but some people are quite comfortable having PITMAN consistently around and he soon becomes a habit.

If he sticks around too long, you are in the danger of becoming a PPP — a **PROFESSIONAL PIT PERSON!**

When we get this serious about being in our PIT, we start renovating. After all if we are planning on being down there for a while we may as well make it comfortable. You see, PPPs like to have a PRETTY PIT!

PPPs put a lot of time into their PIT — they may even get some furniture in, a table, maybe some chairs, a TV and DVD player. (They need the technology to play all of those sad movies and sad songs.)

I mean, if you're going to be a serious PIT DWELLER you might as well do it well! Gee, while you're there, why not render that old red brick wall? Put in some curtains.

Heck, if you're going to be really negative, why not build a basement? Why go up when you can go down deep, really, really deep?

A very seasoned PITMAN approached me after one of my presentations. He said, "I wish my son could hear you speak, he's bloody hopeless! He's 18, unemployed, smokes dope, lies on the couch all day and is just throwing his life away. He is a complete waste of space".

Wow, who's the PITMAN here?

The father of course! I'd say the son is displaying a fair dose of PITMAN behaviour as well, but the father was doing nothing but criticise and beguile his very own son!!

Can you imagine one of the closest people to you telling a complete stranger that you are a waste of space?

I don't know how the father expected me to respond, but I know what I wanted to say. I felt like telling him to get a mirror that works!

Being overly critical is never helpful.

I'm not condoning the son's behaviour, but I am saying that constant criticism is often a contributing factor to keeping an individual in this state.

Let's just pay attention to the language that is used to keep people in the PIT.

How do you react when it rains? When the kids leave their bags at the front door? When the dog poops inside? (My PITMAN comes out when our dog does that!) When the traffic is heavy? When the train is late? When your new lover doesn't call? When your old lover does!

My two boys know all about PITMAN. We can all relate to him. When Jackson is upset with me he will chant in his loudest cranky voice from his bedroom "I love PITMAN! I love PITMAN!"

They know when they go to the PIT and they also know how to get out of it.

I recall sitting beside a gentleman at a conference dinner

at which I had spoken earlier in the day. He said to me that he was really offended when I first started speaking about the PIT.

He thought I was making fun of people who had genuine issues and real struggles in their life, and he questioned, "Who was I to trivialise people like that?"

He then said that the more he listened, the more he realised that I was actually speaking about his wife! He realised that he had climbed into the PIT with her. He felt incredibly sorry for her, yet admitted that he had started finding excuses to work back late because he felt so drained from being around her. He realised that by sympathising with her he was helping her to stay in the PIT.

Wow! What a realization! He was referring to a form of response known as *enabling*.

The point is, when we offer pity to PIT PEOPLE we are not helping them. We are simply reinforcing their reasons to remain in the PIT. I can give you countless stories of people who live their lives in the PIT, either in a rescuing role or as a victim. When we stop rescuing or playing the victim the PIT dance stops.

You need a partner to dance with and while you continue to offer great amounts of pity, attention and sympathy to PIT PEOPLE you give them even more reason to remain in their PIT because you are rewarding them for being a PIT PERSON!

When one of you decides to stop the negative routine, then the other person is faced with a choice. Either learn a new, more positive dance or stay in the PIT and find a new PIT PARTNER.

That's a bit confronting, I hope.

I hear it all the time, from unhappy lovers, discouraged employers and disgruntled employees. I hear it from lots of people who are unhappy with their relationships but are not willing to *do* anything about it.

From painful firsthand experience, I know that you can wait your entire life for someone to get out of the PIT. You can pour out your energy, focus, compassion and effort into "helping" them climb out, only to find years later that little has changed except for the complete depletion of your own energy levels.

There is a wonderful line in a song that goes something like, "How empty of me to be so full of you" which is a brilliant description of how it feels trying to save a PERMANENT PIT PERSON.

After first being offended by my presentation, my dinner companion went on to explain that he had confused empathy with sympathy in his dealings with his wife. This is one of the greatest mistakes we can make when trying to help someone in the PIT.

The difference between empathy and sympathy is this: *sympathy is when you join a person in their dark place (THE PIT) and empathy is when you throw them a ladder!*

TM

© Terry Hawkins 2007

The PIT of misery.

I really don't think we spend enough time understanding the power of empathy and sympathy.

When we sympathise we join them in the PIT and mirror the person's behaviour or mood — if they're sad, we're sad. If they're angry about something, we respond angrily. If they're bitter, we reflect their bitterness. And if they're gossipy, we join in the gossip!

When we empathise instead, we become objective standing back from the situation and in so doing we are being far more helpful.

Sympathy can be seductive and can easily have us in the PIT if we are not careful. Sometimes we even want to throw the doona in and have a PIT PITY day which is fine, as long as we don't get seduced into staying for too long. Remember, it is easy to become stuck in the habit of PIT behaviour.

It's also important to remember that when I talk about PIT behaviour, *I'm not knocking legitimate emotions such as grief and sadness, frustration or appropriate anger.* Life can be tough.

These are not PIT reactions; these are real emotions and are vital for our growth and healing. They are genuine emotions that need to be experienced and expressed.

A good example of the difference between genuine emotion and the PIT comes from a friend of mine. Her husband died tragically in a car accident and a few weeks after, she called me to announce she had gone to the PIT for the night.

She said that she had re-read all the sympathy cards she had received and had a big cry. I told her that this was a really healthy thing to do and she wasn't in the PIT. She was grieving and it was important for her emotional healing to release her feelings.

A few weeks passed and she called me again. This time her conversation went something like this, "I can't cope, I had to drop the kids off to school, deliver a heap of brochures, put the car in for a service, get back to pick up the car in time to get the kids, then they started fighting. It's all too much!"

That's when I said, "Okay, *now* you're in the PIT!"

The PIT is that place we go to when we don't think we have any power. It's where we blame everyone and everything for where we are at in our lives.

When we feel like this, we tend to generate a powerful force that sucks the energy out of anyone who projects a positive outlook.

I know exactly when I'm being a PIT DWELLER, because I can see the effect I have on others. I have less energy, more criticism, quicker anger and less patience. I see it reflected on the faces of those who have to experience my PIT POLLUTION.

I also know how I feel when I'm around PIT DWELLERS. I sometimes feel myself being pulled into their PIT.

While we're on the P, P, P thing...PIT PEOPLE also love to have PIT PARTIES with their PIT PALS. We all know that misery loves company, so PIT PEOPLE tend to hang out together.

They play PIT GAMES, comparing who has had the most miserable life and they almost seem disappointed when they meet someone who has had a worse life than them!

PIT party with PIT PALS.

They totally focus on the negative situations and events in their life, collecting their wounds like badges of honor.

You could call these PERMAMENTLY PROFESSIONAL PIT PEOPLE, *pain-a-holics.* You know the sort — the more wounds the better. Regardless of the positive input they receive, they always add a phrase beginning with "but…"

Don't buy into the drama of the PIT. If you want to throw someone a ladder to get them out of the PIT, then be in an empathic state with them, not in a sympathetic state.

This can be one of the hardest things to do but it shows a much greater love than buying in to their PIT antics. Call it tough love if you wish, but it is the only sensible way to support someone who wants to climb out of their PIT.

Remember, *we* make the decision to take on the role as a PIT PERSON Saviour or a Ladder Thrower.

Sympathy is when you join a person in their dark place (THE PIT) and empathy is when you throw them a ladder!

Chapter **7**

There are no failures in life, just "feedback"

nother time when many of us go to the PIT is when we
receive the kind of "FEEDBACK" that we don't like.
In all my years of studying human behaviour, I have
found that the only time people stretch themselves beyond
their current level is when they receive "FEEDBACK" on
what they're not doing right.

PPPs don't know how to handle "FEEDBACK". They
interpret constructive assistance as a personal attack which
sends them spiraling deeper into their PIT.

So what kind of "FEEDBACK" do we like?

Positive "FEEDBACK" like, "Gosh, you're gorgeous!"

We hate the negative stuff, "I wouldn't sleep with you for practice!"

Positive "FEEDBACK" *is* wonderful, please get this. *We all need to become much better at giving positive "FEEDBACK".*

However, positive "FEEDBACK" only reinforces what we already know about ourselves. It's only when we are shown the "gaps" that we are able to grow. One of the most helpful phrases I have ever heard is: *There are no failures in life, just "FEEDBACK".*

We never ever truly fail in life. We just get "FEEDBACK".

Let's just say your partner leaves you for someone more gorgeous, more wonderful, more stunning, more *everything* than you. Did you fail? No! You just got a little bit of "FEEDBACK".

In moments like these wouldn't it be great to have up your sleeve the line — "Okay honey, have a great life, good luck and oh, thanks for the 'FEEDBACK!'"

Or let's say your business goes broke. Did you fail? No! You just got some "FEEDBACK" on how *not* to run a business next time!!!

And let's say you got the worst possible exam result — did you fail?

No, of course not, you just got some "FEEDBACK". You should have studied harder!

I'm being a bit playful here and we are talking about serious topics. But it really is true that we never, ever fail. Life just gives us "FEEDBACK" on a regular basis.

Adopting this outlook is a healthier and more self-enhancing way to handle the results life serves us. Rather than shrink into the pain of failing, these results give us the opportunity to grow.

When we take such comments on board such as 'failure' instead of "FEEDBACK", we feel sorry for ourselves and often sink into our PIT.

If we accept that every result we get in life is simply "FEEDBACK" (whether it's positive or negative) each will present us with a learning opportunity.

Sometimes a negative result or certain situations and events that occur can bring on many varied reactions such as shock, sadness, grief, anger, despair, denial, humiliation, resentment and so on. It's natural to feel that way. And it's important to experience all these emotions and work through our issues.

But when we make these emotions a habit and constantly remain in a negative state we fall into the danger of being a PERMANENT PIT DWELLER.

Looking at these experiences as nothing more than "FEEDBACK" frees us to move through the emotions so we can find the valuable learnings that come from the events and situations of our life.

If we don't take it on as "FEEDBACK" we can easily become consumed by our reaction. As I mentioned, the PIT is a very seductive place and being miserable can become a habit.

We can also become quite defensive when hearing "FEEDBACK" we don't like. It is not unusual for some people to "shoot the messenger", and in so doing they attack or persecute the person who has been courageous enough to speak up to help them grow.

How did you react last time you received "FEEDBACK" from someone? Did you think about it much? Did you tell anyone about it?

In the initial stages of reception we tend to be too emotional to properly digest all the learnings.

Have you ever called someone immediately after a "FEEDBACK" session to badger them into listening to your complaints about the 'unfairness' of the "FEEDBACK" you got?

"You won't believe what Stacey said about me!"

"I was only 10 minutes late for the meeting!"

"I'm only a day late with my assignment, what's his problem?"

Because we are in a hyper-emotional state the so-called "support" we receive after making such comments can be counterproductive. It can be difficult for us to be logical and to really comprehend what is being said. We react by going into a self protective mode.

Only when we have time to calm down are we able to see the powerful learning opportunities available to us from the experience and maybe start to accept a part of us that we may have denied.

If you want to get maximum benefit from the "FEEDBACK" you receive, simply follow these two key steps:

Step 1.   **Say 'thank you'**
           Be appreciative of the fact that someone cared enough about you to help you grow.

Step 2.   **Wait 24 — 48 hours**

Wait 24-48 hours before discussing the "FEEDBACK" with anyone (especially with someone you care about). This will allow ample time for your emotions to settle and enable you to objectively take the "FEEDBACK" onboard. If, after this time, you still think they're a lunatic, at least you've had time to digest their input objectively.

So, the next time you receive "FEEDBACK", remember, smile and say, "Thank you".

"Feedback" can teach us a lot.

Say 'thank you' after receiving "feedback" and wait 24—48 hours.

Chapter **8**

Don't take this personally, but...

How you deal with "FEEDBACK" is really about choice. Whether you interpret the data positively or negatively depends on the perception you choose to adopt. Whether you see it as a personal attack or an opportunity for growth is subject to you. It's your choice.

But what about all of the other factors that influence our day-to-day moods? How do we go about keeping an optimistic view on life?

Have you ever noticed that when you feel down, rarely does anyone show you *how* to get out of the PIT?

It's a bit like the advice given by well meaning people who say things like, "Don't take your personal problems to work. Make sure you leave them at the front door". (It's easy for them to say!)

But has anyone ever shown you how to *not* take your personal problems to work?

And what about the line, "Don't take this personally" (that invariably precedes personal criticism and is usually followed by the word "but").

One of my friends was recently retrenched. As she was handed the retrenchment letter, her manager said, "Now don't take this personally". She snapped, "I find it very hard not to: the letter starts with the words 'Dear Carol'!"

Wouldn't it be wonderful if we had a formula to avoid taking our personal problems to work?

What if we had a process that enabled us to jump out of that PIT whenever we wanted? Our lives would improve if we were fully empowered to make that choice. If only we had a process where we didn't need an outside influence in order for us to *feel* or *act* in a healthy, positive way again.

Would that be of benefit to you? Would you like to know a process that can enable you to change from being a PIT DWELLER to living a life full of energy?

A lot of us *would* like to live our lives out of the PIT but being a victim has its advantages too! It gives us an out, often providing an opportunity for us to blame others for our problems as well as offering an excuse for why our life isn't working.

The confronting news for really serious PIT DWELLERS

is that when they learn how to live out of the PIT, they can no longer blame others for their problems. That is probably why really serious PIT DWELLERS (the PPPs) don't want exposure to this type of information.

To live outside of the PIT, we must realise that *we* are *personally* responsible for our own lives and that it is *we* who place ourselves in the PIT and *we* are the only ones who can get ourselves out.

It is like a self-renovation. The difference is we're the only one on the site! This is one task we can't delegate.

Sure you can reflect, get advice, read books and attend self-improvement courses but at the end of the day *it is you alone who changes you.*

We have to be the person who takes positive action. No lover, no weight loss program, no job, no house, no child, no school result, no company profit, no friend and no amount of money will get us out of that PIT if we are not willing to climb that ladder ourselves.

Will your support group be waiting for you at the top? Who knows? But we have a much better chance of attracting positive support into our lives if we project positive vibrations.

To be positive people we don't need to be yee-haaaring all over the place. I sometimes cringe when I hear people using the term, *"Positive! Positive! Positive! We've just gotta be positive!"* When I use the word "positive" I am not talking about being a cheerleader who wears rose-coloured glasses. Like all of us, positive people have their limitations.

Positive people sometimes spend time alone in reflection.

Positive people still give themselves the right to experience the entire range of the emotions including, sadness, excitement, grief, joy, anger, despair, disappointment and happiness.

The difference between positive and negative people is that positive people use their limitations to their advantage and to the benefit of others.

Some of the most positive people I have ever met have been quiet, deep thinkers who in their so-called darkest moments have created some of the most amazing outcomes.

On the other hand, some of us think the answer is outside ourselves. We can waste a lot of time and energy waiting for that magical person or event to come along and save us.

We don't realise that the magical answer has been inside of us all along.

So, if you are ready to live a life out of the PIT then keep reading.

Warning!

What follows are a few simple strategies to live a life that allows you to operate from cause, not effect.

That is, being in a place where you take responsibility for how you operate in the world — in contrast to being in a place that consistently blames outside influences for the problems in your life.

I am not saying that you will never go to the PIT again. Of course you will. It's just that after learning the next stage *you* will determine how long you stay there.

Cause: I still go to the PIT occasionally and every time I'm in there, I know it was *me* who put myself there, nobody else.

We are not responsible for how others behave but we are responsible for how we interpret that behaviour and how we react to it.

Effect: Most of us unfortunately exist in a state of blame — *"They did it to me!!"*

Remember the airline attendant at the beginning of this book? She could have blamed Mr. Byrne for upsetting her. She also could have taken her feelings out on other customers. She could have stayed in a bad mood for the rest of the day. She could have let it affect her confidence as well, but she didn't and that had nothing to do with anybody else but her!

She **chose to perceive** the situation differently to PIT People, thus creating a completely different projection to most.

She was completely operating at the level of "Cause".

Use your
limitations
to your benefit.

It is you alone
who changes
you.

Chapter **9**

Perception is projection

There really isn't any such thing as objective reality. How we perceive something — a situation, an event, a person — will determine our interpretation. How we feel then directly affects how we project ourselves.

You project what you perceive.

For example, if you perceive everyone as untrustworthy, waiting to rip you off and hurt you, then you will project a mistrusting, cynical, and guarded attitude.

If you perceive yourself as a confident, loving and enthusiastic person you will project a confident loving and enthusiastic persona.

Life is a mirror. If you see an ugly, negative world then how do you think the world responds?

We are personally responsible for *how* we experience the world. When we take responsibility for our personal projection we will stop blaming others for how we feel.

I remember a woman coming up to me after a presentation and telling me proudly, "Terry, I'm going to the PIT on Saturday!"

"How come?" I replied.

"I've got a huge night planned Friday night and I think I'll be feeling a little untidy the following day!" she said, and we both burst out laughing.

You have to love her honesty and the way she was taking full responsibility for her feelings the 'morning after'. I loved her ownership of the situation. Hey, if you're going to have a PIT DAY, what better way than planning for it?

How often do we hear friends or partners blame each other for their behaviour at a social event?

"Why did you let me drink so much?"

"How could you let me embarrass myself like that?"

"Why didn't you stop me?"

"How could you upset me by behaving like that?"

"Can you imagine what other people thought when you did that?"

So how can we operate from a position that takes full responsibility for how we show up in the world?

How can we get out of that PIT?

How can I get out of the PIT?

We are
responsible for
how we
experience the
world.

You project what
you perceive.

Chapter **10**

Getting out of the PIT

nough of this negative prattle! You now know enough to be able to recognise when you or someone else is using PIT behaviour and language. You also recognise how damaging it is.

Whether it's a few inches deep or all the way to the basement, knowing *how* to get out of the PIT is a powerful and essential tool to enjoying a fulfilled life — that is, the freedom of choice!

Having choice allows you to decide the kind of life you want to live. It doesn't matter how much money you own, what level of education you have, how many friends you enjoy, what job you hold, what has happened in your past or what you look like! ***You are not your past.*** Self judgement and judgment of others is such a PIT way of living.

It amazes me how easily we judge ourselves and others so quickly and so harshly.

Someone once asked whether my audiences ever judge me at public presentations. "Judge me?" I laughed. "They start at my shoes and work their way up! I can see it in their faces."

"Does it worry you?" was the next question.

"No" I replied, "It used to bother me once but now my self esteem is a lot higher".

"You see," I continued, "I am not my hair and I am not my clothes. I am not my shoes and I am not my age. I am not my skin and I am not my sex. The outside of me is what I like to call my 'wrapping paper'. The outside is just how life happened to wrap me up. Terry Hawkins is on the inside."

"We all have different wrapping paper. There are no two people on the face of this planet with the same wrapping paper. Even identical twins are wrapped somewhat differently. The saddest thing I've ever found is when we don't like a person's wrapping paper we don't necessarily bother to find the gift inside."

That's why I can never accept racism. It is completely illogical!

Think about it.

If we were all born blind we wouldn't be racist.

When we judge another person we are really saying a lot more about ourselves than about them.

"I'm not my wrapping paper!"

Personally, I find that I "judge" when I'm feeling insecure. Pay attention to the next time you make someone "wrong" simply because that person lives his or her life differently to you. That's what judgment is to me — seeing another person as being wrong because he or she has chosen a different path. Why are some of us frightened to let others be different to ourselves?

Just as other people are not their wrapping paper, neither are you. There is so much more to all of us than what is on the outside. So don't stay in the PIT just because you feel that someone gave you a good reason to stay there.

Remember, it's all a perception.

None of that matters if you really, truly want to create a future you dream about.

If you have just said to yourself, "You don't know what I've been through!"

HELLO PITMAN!

Remember, we have to pay a price in life. We have to PAY ATTENTION!

If you think this is a whole heap of crap, there is a great saying that reads "Some people are so far behind, they think they're in front". And you know, there are some people who are so far behind that they don't even realise that these comments apply to them!!

Sometimes life feels as though we are locked up in chains. For everyone there comes a time when they need to find the key and unlock the things that inhibit them.

And we all have a villain inside us who has wreaked havoc in our life, we all have a PERSONAL PITMAN!

And, as we know, every villain is usually destroyed by a superhero.

Our very own superhero is STICKMAN!

We all have to
pay a price in life
— and the price
we have to pay is
we have to

pay attention.

Chapter **11**

STICKMAN!

ust as PITMAN lives inside our head, so does STICKMAN.
STICKMAN is the part of us that is powerful, confident,
loved, self assured and successful. When we are in a
STICKMAN state we create far more positive outcomes, take
full responsibility for ourselves and make great choices!

STICKMAN is an amazing and influential figure in the
hundreds of thousands of lives of those who know him. My
life is no exception and everyday I am empowered and
influenced by STICKMAN.

About the only thing STICKMAN and PITMAN have in
common is that we control both of them.

So how does STICKMAN work?

Well STICKMAN is a series of four processes and when we
put them all together we usually create a successful outcome.

I'll start by giving you an overall picture before going into
more detail.

The STICKMAN Process®

Fake it till you make it!

Now, the detail:

The concept of STICKMAN began in my life many years ago. I just didn't recognise who he was then and I hadn't named him yet.

To give you a solid understanding of how powerful STICKMAN is, I would like to outline this part for you in the same way that I learned it.

STICKMAN is a culmination of all that I have learned about human behaviour including Neuro Linguistic Programming (NLP), Emotional Intelligence, Neuro Science and Quantum Physics. This is my interpretation based on these facts.

My aim in creating STICKMAN was to have a simple, powerful analogy that we all can integrate into our daily lives, a character who can support us in creating the life we really want.

Isn't it amazing that there are thousands and thousands of wonderful teachers around us every day, but we can only recognise them if we are paying attention.

When I was about eight years old, I had a grumpy look on my face and my father said to me "Put a smile on your face" and I replied "Well then I'd be lying". He turned to me and said "Sweetheart, I would much prefer one of your fake smiles to one of your sincere frowns!"

Well, of course when you're eight you think, you idiot! But as I got older I realised my father was saying: *FAKE IT, TILL YOU MAKE IT.*

What does "fake it, till you make it" actually mean?

The discovery of the concept of STICKMAN really began

when I wanted to show people *how* to "fake it, till they make it". The answer to this question was the beginning of STICKMAN combined with everything I have learned about the power of the mind and our behaviour.

My passion as a trainer and educator was to help people to *do* (the action), not just to *know* (the theory).

I constantly meet scholars from every sphere of life but do they *do* what they know? Not always.

It was the *doing* that became so powerful for me and the answer to the question, "Do I have to *feel* a certain way in order to *do* the behaviour?" NO!

I wanted to show people *how* to avoid taking personal problems to work, *how* to avoid taking things personally, *how* to avoid letting their past ruin their future. And it's not just talk.

I often hear people saying, "I try to think positively, I try to be happy, I try, I try, I try..."

I remember people reciting affirmations during the 1980s. People thought that all it would take for them to change would be regular recitations of a few positive mantras everyday like, "I'm a powerful, positive, successful human being".

The only problem was so many of them had PITMAN posture, PITMAN projection and PITMAN thinking!

You could walk into their bathrooms and there on the mirror would be a sticker,

SMILE, you're looking at a winner!

This is all well and good, as long as you don't have a screwed up face while you're reading it!

So positive affirmations weren't enough! We needed more. Let me ask you a question, if I were to show someone *how* to fake it till they made it, what would I ask them to *do?*

It took me years to come up with this sentence so please take your time when digesting it. It may sound simple but to be able to execute it we need to understand exactly what this process is.

To be able to *fake it, till you make it*, you need to **fake the opposite positive *behaviour,* thought or feeling to the negative behaviour, thought or feeling you're experiencing.**

Now let's not rush this…it may sound simple but it has many levels.

Once again: If we are to *fake it, till we make it* we need to **fake the opposite positive *behaviour,* thought or feeling to the negative behaviour, thought or feeling you're experiencing.**

I was interviewed for the *Australian* newspaper recently and the interviewer asked me "If you were to tell someone in one sentence how to feel motivated, what would you say?"

"There lies the problem!" I replied. "I aim to run 3 km every day. Do you think that I wake up every day going, 'Yippee! Yippee! Joy! Joy! I'm going for a 3 km run!' No way. Especially on those really cold days, I fight with PITMAN. Sometimes he comes with me all the way on the treadmill — 'Only do 1km today instead of two', he says.

"Have you ever seen the difference between people walking into the gym and the ones walking out? You can hear Saul's *Dead March* playing on the way in and *there's a bluebird on my shoulder...* on the way out.

"People think that they have to *feel* motivated to *do* motivated." I continued. We think we need the feeling in order to do the behaviour, but we don't."

Consider your relationships. As a woman, how often do we wait to *feel* romantic to *do* romantic?

When we don't over-analyse how we "feel about it" and "just do it" it's amazing how enjoyable it can be and I'm sure the words, "We should do that more often!" linger in the bedrooms of many couples. Feelings sometimes catch up with behaviour.

It's the same with work. I constantly say to our team, "We can *feel* sad, we can *feel* tired, we can *feel* miserable or even angry — we just need to *do* happy!"

That's the key — to *do* the behaviour that you *want* to feel. Most of us get stuck in outcomes, as previously discussed.

I want to *be* happy. I want to *be* fit. I want to *be* kind. I want to *be* wealthy.

It's great to have goals but goals are just the outcomes of *doing* the right behaviours.

Change the *be* to *do*. Do happy, do kind, do wealthy, do fit and you'll start to fulfill the behaviours required to achieve these states.

We just need to simplify it enough so we can *do* a behaviour. Take the example of feeling sad: if I were to get you to teach me how to *"fake the opposite positive behaviour to feeling sad"* what would you get me to *do*?

Most people say, 'Smile and think happy thoughts', (I have a friend who can think the happiest thoughts ever yet still *look* sad!).

When we say smile, we're asking the person to *do* an outcome and people can't *do* outcomes, we can only *do* **behaviours**. Smiling *is* the outcome from *doing* a series of behaviours.

Think about that for a moment.

What are the behaviours you need to *do* to change from looking sad to happy (the opposite behaviour) so that the outcome is a smile?

Most of us will just start smiling without stopping to understand what it was that we had to *do* to create that smile.

Take a moment to get this:
When you get this you can create any
***results-producing behaviour* that you want,**
regardless of how you feel.

Let's revisit the original question. How do you fake the opposite positive behaviour to feeling sad?

Let's start with your head — how would it be positioned if you were sad?

Answer: usually hung down — so the first behaviour could be to **lift your head.**

Imagine a sad face. What behaviours would you need to do to that face to make it smile?

- open the eyes
- lift the corners of the mouth
- show the teeth

Do all of those things and you will end up with a happy face!

I can hear all the PIT PEOPLE saying, "That's fine, I might be smiling but I don't *feel* happy."

The wonderful fact about STICKMAN is, if you fake being happy for a while, you will actually start to *feel* happy.

Wow! Can it be that simple? Yes, PIT PEOPLE, it can!

Play a game for me. Take your pointer finger and place it horizontally in your mouth, between your teeth. (So you will need to open your mouth).

PLEASE DO IT!

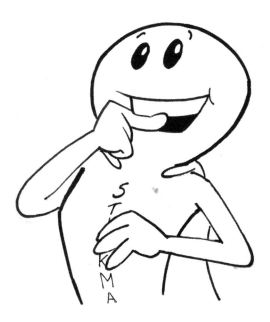

I know it's easy to bypass games like these when we are reading a book but the exercises in this book are the first step in creating change.

Whenever I see the odd person not participating in a game at a conference or in a training program, I know it's because of fear.

They'll tell you it's because they're not going to do anything 'silly' but I know it's because they are so stuck in comfort and control that they won't allow themselves to be vulnerable and they stay stuck in their PIT behaviour!

Now, go on take your finger if you haven't done so, and place it long ways across your mouth.

The moment you did that the corners of your mouth went up; the brain recognised this behaviour and started to release serotonin and endorphins to make you feel better! Fact!

Wow!
And double WOW!

Wouldn't you love to say to some people in your life, "Shove a finger in honey, and get happy!"

That simple exercise really describes the essence of STICKMAN and the four processes required to produce the results we want in our lives.

Fake it till you make it!

Shove a finger in and get happy!!

Chapter **12**

The STICKMAN process

1. The first process is our language — our internal and external dialogue.

Before I go into *how* to do STICKMAN I think it's very important that you realise something: *you already do STICKMAN*. We all do STICKMAN! Let me give you an extreme example.

"I have used STICKMAN to save my life!" an excited voice exclaimed. Standing before me was a beautiful young woman.

"When I was 19," she began, "I was thrown from a horse. I landed on a stick which impaled itself through my abdomen. As I lay on the ground I knew I was in grave danger. This was reinforced by the look on my friend's face that had seen the entire incident."

"'I'll run for help', my friend said with panic in her voice. Knowing it would take a good hour for her to get back I decided to think about my life and how lucky I was to have been so blessed with a wonderful family and great friends."

"I thought that I might die so I decided to relax as much as I could and think about all the experiences for which I was grateful."

"I felt my body slow down and I also noticed a calmness come over me. Later, in hospital, I found out that it was this state of mind and the subsequent response of my body that almost certainly saved my life."

"As I told myself to stay calm and to start breathing in a slow and relaxed manner, the blood flow slowed and minimized the amount of blood loss."

"This ultimately stopped me from going into shock. Terry, as you were describing STICKMAN I realised that this was exactly what I had done that fateful day horse riding. I just never knew what to call it before this!"

What an amazing story! Faced with the same situation, how many of us would have gone straight into panic mode instead?

That's an extreme example, there are countless other day-to-day examples where we have called on STICKMAN even if we didn't know what to call him.

This includes finding the energy to play a game of tennis after a huge day at work or pushing through the "I do not want to keep doing this report...", "Running on this treadmill...", or whatever — how did you get through it?

People say, "I just got a second wind" as if their energy-lift simply happened circumstantially. Well, they didn't literally get a second wind. STICKMAN turned up!

Let's have a look at how this all works. We chat inside of our head all the time. Chat, chat, chat. Most of us are completely oblivious to the conversations that go on between our ears, but if we are to take control of how we react and behave, we MUST listen to this voice.

We all have a price to pay in life and the price is we have to *pay attention*. Shhh, listen...what are you telling yourself right now?

You might be saying "That STICKMAN stuff is interesting, I never looked at it that way before". Or you might be saying, "What's for dinner?". *Whatever you say inside will determine what happens outside.*

As we said before, *perception is projection.*

How you perceive anything determines your reaction to it, emotionally, physically and biologically.

The biggest problem is that most of us don't listen to the talk that goes on inside our heads.

We can easily talk in a way that disenables us and those around us. For example, let's consider the following situation: you have been working hard for a long stretch without a break. You're feeling exhausted, you yawn and say to yourself, "I am so tired".

The moment you say that you see yourself being tired and the second process occurs instantly.

2. The second process is that your Unconscious Mind accepts this language as truth.

Your unconscious mind instantly confirms whatever you tell yourself. This is because your unconscious mind doesn't know the difference between fact and fiction.

It believes everything you tell it. This is why it is crucial to pay attention to the actual language you use.

Take for example, relationships.

It's so easy to sledge your partner. How damaging do you think it is to the relationship when the one or both parties think that sarcastic quips are a form of humour?

Sarcasm requires making a joke at someone else's expense. And even after the "Sorry, only joking honey" has come-and-gone the damage has been done. That moment has been recorded in the unconscious mind forever.

So even 20 years into a relationship you may be surprised to hear a couple say, "I don't know why, we just don't love each anymore." Yet the unconscious mind is screaming, "I know the reason — it's because we say all of those horrible things to each other!"

And we wonder why we fall out of love?

The third process occurs immediately after the unconscious mind receives the language.

3. In the third process the body aligns itself to the Unconscious Mind and its language.

Whatever dialogue occurs, the unconscious mind has to be congruent with the body, and so it aligns itself.

Let's put all this together:

Process 1. Language
You say "Gee I'm tired!"

Process 2. The unconscious mind then accepts this as truth.
It says "You know far better than I do, so I believe you", at which point it sends a message directly to the body.

Process 3. The body then aligns itself to the unconscious mind and the language.
It creates a biological response that produces feelings of being sluggish and slow.

The STICKMAN Process®

Fake it till you make it!

Okay, now that we understand the process of STICKMAN let's go back to how we *do* STICKMAN. You fake the opposite positive behaviour to the negative emotion you're experiencing.

So, you will need to ask yourself "What is the opposite positive behaviour of being tired?" ALIVE! AWAKE! ENERGISED!

Do you really feel alive, awake and energised? Emphatically not! Does your unconscious mind know that? No — because it believes everything that you tell it.

In the initial stages of developing STICKMAN, I thought all I needed to do was go around telling myself, "I'm awake, I'm alive, I'm a Happenin' Girl!" And nothing happened!

Nothing happened because I was missing one vital part — Process 4. I will get to this vital link shortly.

However, before I do, it might be worthwhile to give you a few examples of how powerful this process can be.

Let's take some basic examples that everyone can relate to.

Do you know anyone who bites their nails? Well, I was a very competitive little miss in the days when I was a nail biter. Nail biting was something I had done for as long as I could remember. I was the queen of nail biters!

I came into our lounge room one day and there sat my son Harison, having a good chew on his nails (he was about 3½ at the time). I said, "Stop biting your nails" to which he replied, "Why? You do it!"

As I am not one of those parents who support the "Do as I say, not as I do" theory, I said, "Thanks for the "FEEDBACK!", but I knew right then I had to stop biting my nails while Harison was still in the zero to seven age group because ages seven and under are the most crucial time for the development of our children's belief systems. Children are so influenced at this age I knew that whatever I *did* would impact on him heavily. To beat the habit I had to work through the STICKMAN processes.

1. First, I needed to change my languaging. What is the opposite (positive) behaviour to the (negative) state of nail biting? The trick here is to focus on the result that you want, then language it as if you already have it.

Let's read that again slowly. It is such an important paragraph:

The trick here is to focus on the result you want, then language it as if you already have it.

Think about this carefully: a lot of us rush in and say something like "Stop biting your nails".

Look at that statement.

The unconscious mind focuses on the behaviour not the command. So when you say Stop — (command) biting your nails (behaviour), your mind has to first make a picture of biting the nails. And once that picture is created, the unconscious mind thinks that is what you want to do.

Another example is when you pour a child a glass of milk, almost habitually you say, "Now, don't spill the milk". No sooner are the words out your mouth than milk is all over the floor. "I specifically told you not to spill the milk!" The child thinks "Wow, she's a clairvoyant."

So what happened? When you said "Don't spill the milk" the child had to make a picture of spilling the milk in his or her mind, in order not to (by which time it's too late). The unconscious mind received the data, the body aligned and whammo, milk was everywhere.

It's the same when people use language such as "I'll never be able to stop smoking" — listen to that! The unconscious mind just goes "Okay, you know far better than I do".

It's the same with expressions like, "I always..." or "I can't...". We're not allowed to say "I can't" in our house. You must say "I am" or "I have" instead. "I have long, healthy nails! I have long healthy nails! I have long healthy nails!"

Focus on the end result that you want and then language it as if you already have it — "I AM..." "I HAVE..."

Whatever you
say inside
will determine
what happens
outside.

Chapter **13**

Don't say
'I can't', say
'I AM!'

I recall Harison walking into the kitchen when he was four years old. He was slumped over (in the PIT) saying "I can't find Thomas the Tank mama, I can't find Thomas!" I knelt down to his eye level and said "Harison, we don't say I can't in this house, we say…?"

But before I could finish, he jumped in with "I *am* finding Thomas, I *am* finding Thomas." After I'd left the room I could hear him searching in his toy box chanting, "I *am* finding Thomas, I *am* finding Thomas."

Next, there was a squeal of delight, followed by "I found him!" And then I asked, "How was that?" "Worth it" he shouted back. That was to encourage him to keep persisting at things and to make sure that he doesn't become a quitter. (My poor kids, I'm sure I'll do their heads in!)

Jackson is a little different to Harison. I remember when he was three years old he was having trouble doing up his buttons.

"I can't do up my buttons mama, I can't do up my buttons", I responded with the usual line "We don't say I can't, we say...?"

He leapt in with a very angry voice and shouted at the top of his lungs, *"No I am! I said I can't!"* Languaging can have its' funny moments. I had a bit of a chuckle and thought we'll wait awhile for this little guy.

Another story that comes to mind was when Jackson was looking for his huggy in his bedroom (the little security blanket he had since birth).

Next thing he shouted out, "Mama, I can't find my huggy, I keep saying 'I *am* finding my huggy, I *am* finding my huggy' — but I just can't find it!"

I replied with a chuckle, "That's because it's in the car!"

I can hear some of you from here, saying, "Well that's all fine and good with something as simple as nail biting (tell that to a nail biter!) or looking for a toy truck, but I just can't quit smoking.

I too was like that. I'd think, "Why smoke .05mg cigarettes when you can have a Camel with no filter instead?" I was a very committed smoker!

I would smoke as fast as I spoke and sometimes I'd have one resting on the ashtray while lighting another.

It didn't matter how much I tried, it seemed as if these little white sticks had complete control over me. My father died from lung cancer at 48 years of age.

When you're 15, 48 seems an eternity away, but as you get older you realise just how young that really is. As for the belief systems that form between the years of zero to seven — five out of my father's six children became heavy smokers!

I never thought I would ever be able to quit smoking and I used to fear that I would end up with lung cancer like my father.

Isn't it amazing how life has a wonderful way of helping you out if you PAY ATTENTION?

Remember we have to pay a price in life and the price we have to pay is that we have to pay attention. Shhh, listen to the messages life brings you.

If you need to get a lesson in life, then life will give you a little tap on the shoulder to capture your attention. Life doesn't want us to experience great pain in our learning but if we're not paying attention, then it will get our attention, any way it can!

If we don't respond to the tap, we'll get a slap. If we don't pay attention to the slap, then we'll get a punch. If we don't pay attention to the punch then it will be a sledge hammer and if we're still not listening, a Mack Truck will come along and smack us fair and square in the face and say, "**Now will you listen!**"

Think about it — when do most of us decide to get our health on track? When we get a health scare.

When do most people read books about relationships? That's right, when their partner has packed and is headed out the door. We turn the pages of the book and acknowledge, "Hmm, so that's what went wrong".

For most people the Mack Truck experience is a crisis situation. For me, I met four people in one week who had throat cancer. The last person was a woman who came up to me in a coffee break, during one of our training programs.

She grabbed my arm and said with a mixture of fear and tears, "Terry, put that stupid cigarette out! My husband has just been diagnosed with cancer of the duodenum".

Well, you could have knocked me over with a feather. In that moment I knew I would never again have another cigarette. I just 'woke up'.

It's the best way that I can describe my experience and since then have found out that experience is called SATORI — instant awakening!

It was as if all the lights had been turned on for me in that one moment. WOW! But then I thought "Now that I've made this powerful decision, how on earth am I going to quit these horrid things?"

Then I remembered STICKMAN!

Yay! STICKMAN will help me through!

I remember being confronted with the fear that STICKMAN mightn't be enough. What if he didn't work for me after all this time I'd spent preaching about him to others?

The wonderful thing about STICKMAN is that you don't have to believe in him to succeed. You just have to *do* the required behaviours.

So let's work through this one together...this is The STICKMAN Process™ which helps create the results that you want.

Firstly, what could be a positive behaviour that would combat my negative feelings, thoughts or visuals of wanting a cigarette?

(Careful not to slip back into old languaging habits e.g. Don't smoke! Stop smoking! Remember the unconscious mind makes a picture of the behaviour.)

Tip: Though you're not actually there yet, think about where you want to end up. Some people might say, "A non-smoker with healthy, pink lungs". These are outcomes.

What languaging will help me get there? What feeling do I need to have, what picture do I need to make and what dialogue do I need to hear to support me in this outcome?

If you're struggling for an answer, I'm thrilled. It means that you're beginning to realise that the formula might sound easy, yet it's not quite so easy to put into practice.

We really don't spend enough time focusing on our languaging. We pay insufficient attention to the bad thinking and speaking habits that we pick up along the way.

We don't realise the damage that can be done through fostering such habits. When we create the new language, it needs to be a behaviour that will support us through our most tempting moments.

So, let me ask you, "What do non smokers hate?"

No, they don't hate other smokers. (Love the criminal, hate the crime!) They hate the smell of cigarette smoke.

So, using a negative auditory stimulus I **told** myself "The smell of cigarettes makes me sick".

Then using a negative visualization I **pictured** myself being physically sick when I smelt cigarette smoke (the more visual the better). I would imagine a **feeling** of nausea when I smelt it (kinesthetic stimulus).

So off I went with my new mantra, "The smell of cigarette smoke makes me sick, the smell of cigarette smoke makes me sick, the smell of cigarette smoke makes me sick..." added to which I imagined a nauseous feeling and pictured myself throwing up.

Well, do you think it made me sick for the first few weeks?

Not in your life! For the first few weeks I would walk past a smoker hoping they would breathe out when I breathed in — mmm, beautiful!

But inside my head I persisted with my mantra. "The smell of cigarette smoke makes me sick, the smell of cigarette smoke makes me sick, the smell of cigarette smoke makes me sick..." because my unconscious mind didn't know any different.

About six weeks later after landing from a midnight to dawn flight, I walked out of Sydney Airport and walked past a group of smokers at the door. I took in a breath and felt physically sick — at last! I even dry retched!

Let me tell you, I did a happy dance all the way to the car. "The smell of cigarette smoke makes me sick — yee har!" It was music to my ears.

To this day the smell of smoke continues to make me sick and I love that feeling.

My partner and I were at a dinner party a couple of years after I had stopped smoking and after eating way too much, one of the guests lit up a cigarette. PITMAN circled around me whispering "Gee it would be nice to have a cigarette right now!" Aagh, PITMAN!

He was trying to sneak back in, "One won't hurt you. Just have *one*, you'll be okay". No, PITMAN you will not get back in!

"THE SMELL OF CIGARETTE SMOKE MAKES ME SICK", I said loud and clear just to be sure not one little urge leaked its way back in. Yuk, gag!

You see, we have to pay a price in life, that's right, we have to PAY ATTENTION!

But this is not a story about me, and it's not about smoking or nail biting — it's a story about you and about anything in your life that is stopping you from moving forward.

I am not telling you to quit smoking and nor am I judging smokers. Do whatever you want to do but when you are ready to make any changes to your life, STICKMAN will help.

It's a bit like drinking alcohol. I would come home from work in the evening and have a glass, two glasses sometimes more than that. People would ask me, "How much do you drink a night?" I would answer, "I only have a glass at night, it's not my fault it's shaped like a bottle!"

It was really a bit like lolly water to me and I would tend to drink as fast as I spoke! Jokes aside, I really was a bit of a guzzler! I cut down a lot after having my babies so that over recent years I was only drinking a couple of glasses of wine mixed with soda. But I still needed those couple of glasses.

Looking back, I can honestly say that I consumed a great deal of alcohol since I started drinking at 18, as I'm sure a lot of readers have.

When my brother died at the age of 43 from alcohol-related liver failure, I was strongly convinced to do something about my personal habits. Just like smoking, it seemed impossible to contemplate a life without alcohol. I found myself really needing those couple of glasses each evening.

Yet there was something deep inside telling me that alcohol was incompatible with my life goals.

As luck would have it (this was my sledgehammer) a few years ago I went to see a doctor because I wasn't feeling in top gear. She ran a few tests and discovered that I had quite a serious parasite.

"I can't have," I laughed. "That old boyfriend left years ago!" She laughed too, but then said that she was very concerned about my condition and recommended that I undergo a heavy course of antibiotics. She then added that because of the high dosage, I was not to drink alcohol for four whole weeks!

It was like slow motion. "Hooooow looooooong did you say?" I asked, hoping that I'd misheard and the doctor had really said four hours!

"Four weeks" she said firmly.

"What? Four whole weeks!" I found this all very confronting.

I kept weighing it up. Drinking — parasite — drinking — parasite — maybe if I drank enough alcohol, I would kill the parasite! I really was confronted by the choice that lay before me — my health or alcohol — and I found it a very difficult choice to make.

Even though I knew deep down I would ultimately choose my health, I was angry that I had to give up something for four weeks that I enjoyed and felt I needed. I didn't know my adult life without alcohol.

It sounds pathetic, doesn't it? But when anything has a hold of you it can be very hard to let it go, even if it isn't good for you.

I have to tell you, this was an incredibly confronting situation. My liver was not as healthy as it should have been and my brother's death was a pretty strong influence on my giving up on alcohol. In the end of course, I chose my health.

The hardest part for me in stopping the consumption of any alcohol was the first four weeks. I even held a ceremonial dinner the night before I quit.

Day one was tough, day two was worse, day three got a little easier and as each day went on I felt myself gaining new strength. The four weeks were over before I knew it and I must say I felt a lot better for my restraint.

Not only had my skin tone dramatically improved, but my mental clarity had never been sharper!

Encouraged by this renewed strength, I decided to persist

along my course of abstinence. I didn't know how I would fare so I didn't put any pressure on myself. I decided that if I really felt like a drink I would simply have one. Initially my language was "I'm not drinking because I'm taking medication" which I changed to "I'm off alcohol at the moment".

My last alcoholic drink was at 9.30pm on the 9th August 2003. Now when I'm asked, I simply reply that I only drink non alcoholic drinks.

At this point in my life, I never see myself drinking alcohol again. Do I miss it? No. I am amazed at how easy it has been to completely stop — although I do admit that in the early days there was the occasional evening when I felt that a long glass of icy cold champagne would have slid down beautifully.

I am not suggesting that we should have an alcohol-free world. I am only speaking for myself here. I am simply not good with alcohol. Alcohol doesn't work for me.

My greatest realisation was that drinking numbed me. I didn't need to face my "stuff". My problems and issues became less important after a couple of glasses. Alcohol became like a sedative. I lived a lot of my life in a haze (which of course I didn't realise until I stopped drinking). When I did stop drinking, everything I had been pushing down came up. I was now faced with the ordeal of dealing with it.

But now that I had a clear head, the most amazing thing was how much easier it was for me to deal with the very issues I was drinking to avoid.

Again, I am not saying to you "don't drink" — you might have a completely different constitution to mine. Being a non drinker is a great choice for me because I didn't like who I became when I drank. You may be completely different. Be totally honest with yourself. Deep down there is a part of you that knows the truth. It knows whether you're using a substance to push away whatever you're running from.

When we use anything to numb ourselves from the reality of our own issues, (food, drugs, alcohol, anger, work, chocolate, etc,) we're not getting rid of problems — we're just pushing them down. The moment we stop the habit, up they come!

Unfortunately, thousands and thousands of people are on antidepressants because of that very reason. Their "stuff" comes up and rather than face the pain, discomfort and fear they numb it through alcohol or prescription or illegal drugs.

I think that the saddest part of our current society is that we don't let our "stuff" come up, whatever the stuff may be.

Don't say 'I can't', say 'I AM!'

Chapter **14**

The quick fix

*W*e've turned into a society that wants a quick fix, we want a pill to make us happy when we're sad, a pill to make us relax when we're stressed, a pill to make us sleep, a pill to keep us awake, a pill to help us lose weight, a pill for this and a pill for that.

Believing that the weight drops off while you sleep, I was one of those nutters who sent $400 to an American company to buy diet pills to take before going to bed!

Hello?

I was about 7-8kg over my normal weight and rather than kick my butt out of bed each morning to do some exercise, I wanted the easy way out. Why was I the only idiot to not realise this just couldn't work?

Guess what I discovered? I discovered that there is no easy way to accomplish challenging goals.

LIFE IS CHALLENGING! Being a parent is challenging, being married is challenging, being single is challenging, being 15 is challenging, being 50 is challenging, running a company is challenging, running 3km is challenging, LIFE IS CHALLENGING!

There are no free lunches in this world.

When we start to accept that life is challenging, everything begins to get easier. We stop looking for an easy way out and accept that there is work to be done.

Many years ago I wasn't sleeping very well because my ex husband was a big snorer. After quite a few weeks of sleep deprivation I felt exhausted.

I also had an extremely painful right elbow, which would work in tandem with the snoring to ensure that some nights I had entirely no sleep.

All of this plus I was working full time with two little boys (I sound like a bit of a PITMAN, don't I?). I dragged myself off to the doctor in search of a remedy for my lack of sleep. By this stage I was very teary, a bit spacey and felt like I had been hit by a truck!

After approximately 15 minutes of consultation the doctor prescribed antidepressants. I had no reason to be depressed. "Why?" I questioned in shock. I had a loving marriage, two great toddlers, a fulfilling business and I was happy with my life. "I certainly don't feel depressed!"

The doctor replied, "I think you're not sleeping because you're depressed."

I was absolutely dumbfounded by this diagnosis. So I clarified what he'd said.

"You're saying I'm not sleeping because I'm sad, is that right?"

"Yes," he confidently replied.

"Might it be the other way around? That I'm sad because I am not sleeping?" I said through gritted teeth.

He became quite irritated that I had questioned his diagnosis. And I was annoyed that he prescribed antidepressants so casually, without discussing my diet, exercise or lifestyle. He knew nothing about my personal life or anything else about me, full stop!

Back then my attitude to exercise was simply, "Why walk when there's a good car parked outside!" And there he sat, happy to tell me that I needed antidepressants, while offering no other form of therapy or relief for my sleeplessness.

(And I am not saying that there isn't a place for antidepressants. If they're going to prevent someone from taking their own life or if they're going to give someone a jolt from a continual PITMAN state, then I say go for it, but they shouldn't be prescribed this casually.)

I walked out of his surgery sad and when I had a chance to clear my head I questioned, "How dare anyone so easily play with my body like that?"

I've had 17 year old girls tell me they have been on antidepressants for years.

(I wonder how many tell the doctor they're coming down from a party drug they took the night before. Some party drugs inhibit the body's ability to produce endorphins — so there's the chemical imbalance!)

Another reason some teenagers are prescribed anti-depressants is because they think there is something wrong with them when in actual fact most of them just don't understand the changes that are going on with their bodies or their brains.

When a teenager reaches puberty the brain starts to re-wire itself.

Studies have recently shown that there is the same, if not more, re–wiring done at this age than there is in the first three years of their life!

In the course of the re-wiring process teenagers lose 75 per cent of their reasoning power which doesn't fully return until around the age of 19.

So...*it is normal for a teenager to be confused!*

It's normal *for them* to be testing boundaries, it's normal *for them* to experiment sexually and perhaps even with drugs, it's normal *for them* to sometimes let a blemish ruin their lives, it's normal *for them* to be thrown into the depths of depression when rejected by a potential love interest.

All of this is *normal* for teenagers because they are only operating with 25 per cent of their reasoning power. If they were totally rational they would see why boundaries are necessary, and they would understand the risks involved in casual sex and drug abuse. And as for that love interest, they would realise that they will almost certainly have many loves in their life not just this one, and that really is only a pimple that WILL clear.

This is one of the reasons I enjoy speaking to high school students about PITMAN and STICKMAN. This gives them a strategy to help get them through those difficult teen years.

As they start to understand who they really are, what their values are and who they can become they also start to understand that this confusion is all part of their journey. They also realise that when they go to the PIT, it's not forever.

Unfortunately for many teenagers this is not always the case. Way too many go to the PIT and think that's the way their life is going to remain. This can result in feeling an inability to cope and in the worst case scenario, lead to teenage suicide, (which is on the rise).

Let me give a couple of examples of emails I have received from some of these amazing people:

119

Hello Terry,

My name is Joshua* and I was at the college when you gave your talk. I would just like to thank you personally, you have changed my life for the better and probably stopped me doing something really stupid. I have contemplated suicide about four times, and it scared me shitless, I probably wouldn't have gone through with it anyway, but what normal person even thinks about doing a thing like that? And it was not until your talk, that I realised how completely and utterly stupid that is! I have not felt any tendency like that ever since your talk, I can almost say with complete confidence that ultimately you have saved my life! I am not sure how I can thank you, you are a beautiful person, and a wonderful role model, I wish there were more people like you! Now instead of walking around with a face that reflected my suicidal thoughts, I walk with a smile and a head full of positive thoughts, and I have also learned to revere life, and those I love much much more! So thank you so much Terry, for making my mornings bearable and my days beautiful,

Joshua, 14 years.

* The names have been changed for anonymity

Dear Mrs. Hawkins,

Firstly I would like to say how much you have helped me, with the outstanding speech that you presented at my high school. My name is Suze and I am currently in grade 11. Your speech was spectacular. It made me wake to everything in life. My Grandma of 77 years passed away last year. This was a result of cancer. Even though she had received three sessions of chemotherapy, it worked in the opposite way. Instead of reducing the cancer it actually made it grow. My Grandma and I were extremely close, and this just absolutely shattered me. Even though I had seen Grandma the night before she passed away, I still feel like I could have said so much more. Saying goodbye to Grandma the next day was extremely hard but very helpful at the same time. I personally think I was the most caring grandchild. I loved and cherished her with everything I had. And hurt me lots. I was at the hospital every day seeing Grandma, and on weekdays after school whenever I had the chance.

I was the PIT Man up until you came and visited our school, which is why I am writing you this email. What you explained about PIT Man is what was happening to me. Your talk was so helpful. I have been drunk before, and the story about your brother made me wake up to myself. I thought, do I really want to throw my life away and risk being an alcoholic? Hell no. I'm sorry if I am offending you in any way. So I don't drink and never will ever again. These are just a couple of things you helped me with. Whenever I am feeling like I want to be PIT Man, I can simply say no. You have also inspired me to achieve everything, and that nothing is impossible, which is why I make the most of everything that I do.

I can not thank you enough. Thank you for everything.

Yours faithfully
Suze*, 16 years.

Wow! What an amazing couple of people! And I have received hundreds of emails with similar stories. I can barely get through them without tears streaming down my face. Tears of joy! Joy that these powerful, courageous people have taken responsibility for their own lives. Joy that at such a young age they have learned who controls their life — they do!

I think teenagers are amazing!

While their bodies and brains are undergoing massive change they have to deal with parents who are frequently more confused than they are. Then they use all their leftover energy to focus on school and homework and then, hopefully after all of that, get a good result. I don't know many adults who could cope as well under such levels of pressure!

It is so important to encourage teenagers by reinforcing that they are *not* their high school result. It is just a piece of paper and will not determine the rest of their life.

If they didn't do well at school they should simply accept it as "FEEDBACK" from which they can learn a lesson — probably that they should have studied harder. Accept it, and then get on with life! When asked about this I reply that if they don't get the result they had hoped for they can always go back to study and get it another way. A high school is not the only way.

I created PITMAN because of two teenagers who killed themselves after receiving their high school leaving results. I knew them, in fact I had worked with them some months previously.

Life is hard, I was devastated when I heard the sad news. I needed to find a model to communicate how it feels in that miserable, downhearted PIT.

I want people, especially teenagers, to recognise when they are down there — but more importantly, I want them to realise that there *is* a way out. There is a wonderful saying, "This too shall pass" and it always does.

If STICKMAN can help just one person make a better choice to live the life he or she was meant to live, then it will have been worth all my effort.

The mail I have received from teenagers who have embraced STICKMAN and created significant change in their lives is overwhelming and astounding.

These "giants" are living proof that STICKMAN can provide a solution from bad habits like nail biting, binge drinking and even saying no to suicide!

I know that there will be some skeptics who will say, "I'm not convinced it will work. Losing my anxieties can't be that easy and changing your life can't be that simple?"

I say it is. We just have to get out of our own way. We already know that STICKMAN is scientific fact! So we have every reason to accept him.

If you're not ready for him yet, that's okay too. Just know that when you are, STICKMAN will be there, waiting to help you.

Let's see how all of this comes together.

When we start to accept that life is challenging, everything begins to get easier.

Confusion always precedes a higher state of learning.

Chapter **15**

The missing link

Process 1.   Language example:
              You say "Gee I'm tired!"
Process 2.   Your unconscious mind accepts this as truth.
              It says, "You know far better than I do, so I
              believe you" at which point it sends a message
              directly to the body.
Process 3.   The body then aligns itself to the unconscious
              mind and the languaging
              It creates a biological response that produces
              feelings of being sluggish and slow.

The fourth process really brings it all together. In order
to break the habit-cycle I have to take action. I have to *do*
process four. For example to create long healthy nails, I have
to keep my fingernails out of my mouth. To quit smoking

I must put the cigarette out and to stop drinking I have to put the drink down.

I have to LIVE IT!

The STICKMAN Process®
Fake it till you make it!

Process 4.   LIVE IT!

Here we must *do* the language of Process 1. We must live the language. Live it, breath it, walk it, talk it!

This is the *take action* part of STICKMAN.

Let's put Process Four into practice and use the earlier "I'm tired" example. We now replace "tired" with "awake, alive, and energised". As we have discovered, just saying the words isn't enough.

We have to let the body know we're there, even if we don't feel it yet.

It's like we're tricking our brain — remember the unconscious mind believes everything we tell it.

So how do we *do* alive, awake and energised?

We walk faster; we hold our head upright; we adopt a strong posture; we keep our eyes wide open; we have a strong positive voice projection ... and so on

So, when you bring it all together we,

SEE IT, SAY IT, FEEL IT, DO IT!

SEE IT! –   make a visual of your desired outcome
SAY IT! –   language your desired outcome
FEEL IT! – imagine how you will feel when you achieve your desired outcome
DO IT!   Take action ... do what needs to be done to achieve the desired outcome.

I meet a lot of people who use the right languaging which is great! But nothing will happen unless they go even further — and live it.

It's a bit like the phrase, "I love you". Love is a verb, it's a doing word.

We say, "I love my kids more than anything in the whole world" yet we get really cross with them because they want to talk during the evening news.

Some people say, "I love my family!" yet they spend 80 per cent of their waking moments at the office.

We say, "I want to be a great salesperson" but we won't allow ourselves to overcome the discomfort of being rejected.

We say, "I want to be fit!" yet we stay in bed and miss our morning workout.

We say, "I want to treat people with respect" yet we lose our temper or judge them harshly.

We say, "I want to achieve great things in my life" yet we won't *do* what it takes to get there.

We say, "I want to save my marriage" yet we don't want to alter our destructive behaviours.

The truth is you already *do* STICKMAN. Picture this.

You are walking to your car after work, feeling exhausted and the only soothing thought is a long hot bubbly bath waiting for you at home.

Brrrring! It's your mobile.

You think, "I'd better answer it." In an exhausted voice, you flick it on and say,

"Yeah, who is it?"

"Hi, it's Gary! Do you feel like going out to the club for a few drinks?" (Your pace quickens slightly) "The whole gang will be there!"

Suddenly everything has changed, you're revitalized, and you start running to the car.

"I'll be there in 20 minutes" you say excitedly and by 10pm there you are, dancing around that pole!!

People say to me, "I got a second wind" — well that so-called second wind was STICKMAN! You felt exhausted a few moments before but by simply changing your languaging and behaviour, you felt full of energy.

The easiest way to feel different is to *do* a different behavior. Walk faster, use quicker motions. If you're feeling lethargic, *do* energy by *acting* in an energetic way.

If you're feeling sad — smile and sing a happy song.

People don't sing because they're happy, they're happy because they sing.

It is important and also healthy to be in touch with all of our emotions and to fully express our feelings. I'm not saying that we should suppress our true emotions or pretend to feel something we don't feel.

However, **it is not always appropriate to express our emotions in the moment.** We've all been served by someone who decided to truly express their emotions — the grumpy bank teller, the cat's bum-face checkout operator, the rude shop assistant, the indifferent sales consultant, etc, some people make excuses for their attitude by saying they don't like their job.

I say give it all you've got till something better comes along. Do your best.

At the end of a big day I don't always feel like having loads of energy for two little boys, but I can *do* energy.

I see STICKMAN everywhere, especially at sporting venues. When our team wins, we punch the air and scream!

Can you imagine punching the air and letting out a huge scream when you were in the PIT? You would really trick the unconscious mind then, wouldn't you?

The body would start producing lots of feel-good chemicals and before you knew it, you would be buzzing again.

The trouble is PITMAN starts whispering in our ear and saying things like "You don't feel like punching the air. You don't feel like being happy. You feel miserable".

DON'T LISTEN!

Don't ask yourself how you feel, just do it! Success is not about what you feel. It's about what you do, regardless of how you feel.

Successful people continue to do whatever it takes, regardless of what they may be feeling. And they don't make other people pay for their emotional fluctuations.

Adopting STICKMAN is a way to kill PITMAN. And we make the choice to be the best "me" on offer every moment of every day.

That choice is totally dependent on our perception of the situation. It is not dependent on anything or anyone outside of us. STICKMAN gives us the power to make that choice.

Over the years I have heard countless stories from people who have shared how STICKMAN has influenced their life. From weight loss to quitting smoking; from saving a person's life to becoming the number one salesperson in the firm; people have shown me that STICKMAN lives in the choices we make each moment.

At a client function, I ran into someone whom I had trained a few years back in our C.A.R.E™ program. She excitedly wanted to share a story about her final exam to qualify as a firefighter.

"A building was on fire, my partner was inside. My task was to find my partner and get him out of the burning building. This was my last task before becoming a fully qualified fire fighter. I had trained so hard for this moment."

"I only had a certain amount of time and for some reason the heat, the pressure, the race against time started to have a negative affect on me. I started to panic. My breath became short, I couldn't find my partner, and I felt like I was burning up, it was awful. I was about to give in and give up when I remembered STICKMAN!"

You should have seen the look on her face as she shared her story. I had goose bumps on my arms and tears in my eyes.

"I knew that if I just focused on STICKMAN I would be okay. I was still terrified but I concentrated on slowing my breathing. In, out, in, out. My heart was pounding so hard I thought it was going to burst through my chest. I kept breathing in, out, in, out. I then clearly visualised myself finding my partner.

"I started moving forward into the fire, saying out loud, **I *am* finding my partner! I *am* finding my partner!** Within what felt like a few seconds, my partner appeared before my eyes. We got out of that fire and I passed my test! I love STICKMAN!" she yelled as we fell into a beautiful hug.

That story shook me for ages. I love STICKMAN too, the number of situations where he turns up never ceases to amaze me.

STICKMAN doesn't only have to be there for us in life threatening situations, he can also be with us in ordinary stressful day-to-day situations.

Remember, STICKMAN is about what we *do*, not what we feel. I'm not saying we should avoid our feelings, but it's not always appropriate to express everything we feel nor is it smart to make other people pay for our mood swings.

We sometimes feel frustrated when driving in traffic and we have a choice — either (1) get even with the driver who cut us off or (2) drop the agro and *do* relaxed.

After a hard day's work I bet you sometimes get cranky with the kids when you get home. Remember, you can either *do* "tired" or you can *do* "patient, interested and kind". It's up to you.

You may feel bored and disgruntled with your work or you can *do* interested and enthusiastic.

You may feel tired and disinterested in your partner or you can *do* passionate and loving.

You may feel revengeful and hateful or you can *do* forgiveness and understanding.

I know this may sound difficult but doing the behaviour is probably easier than feeling it, and the more you do it the quicker you feel it!

Now when I'm feeling angry I find it much easier to do kindness because I've had a lot more practice. It used to be the other way round.

It still blows me away when I hear people complaining about an aspect of their life without doing anything to make it more positive.

Someone once said to me, "My relationship is in the toilet" and I replied, "What have you done about it?"

"Nothing," she answered.

So I said, "Flush!"

If nothing changes, nothing changes. *You don't have to feel a behaviour to do a behaviour*. If we wait until we *feel* like doing something different we will probably be waiting a very long time.

Remember, it's all in the *do!*

If you don't like what you're doing, then change it.

Why complain about a problem that you're not going to do anything about? Why would you buy the bus ticket and then bitch about the bus ride? It's exactly that way with the people who bitch about their work.

Every day we make the choice about where and how we will spend our day. We decide if we want to be a STICKMAN and when we do we become far more aware of the PIT PEOPLE around us.

It can also be hard to resist the temptation of judging them.

I hope nobody reads this book, walks up to the first energy sucker he or she knows and says, "Hey PITMAN, I've got some "FEEDBACK" for you!"

I'm sure you realise that this is about *us* working on our *own* "stuff". When we're criticising someone else's backyard, we're usually growing weeds in our own! And that's PITMAN stuff.

Use it for good, not evil!

The quickest way to feel
different is to *do* different

SEE IT!

SAY IT!

FEEL IT!

DO IT!

Chapter **16**

Use it for good, not evil!

t is important to use this information as positively as you can. It can be counter-productive to label someone a PITMAN and who are we to judge that anyway? So, I don't suggest that you walk up to the people in your life who are having a PIT moment and say "HEY PITGIRL, I've got some "FEEDBACK!" for you!!!" I'm not sure you'll get a positive response. (That's a bit like "cup drilling" which I'll come to.)

You may also have the best of intentions to "save" the PIT PEOPLE in your life but you must remember that no one can help you when you are in your PIT.

It is our choice, our languaging, our behaviour that places

our foot on that first rung. For now, the best thing we can do is to "get this" for ourselves. *The best way to teach is to do.*

Be the person you want your kids, your lover, your boss, your staff, your friends, your teammates to be.

Be a more loving and respectful parent if you want more loving and respectful kids.

Be a present and attentive partner if you want the same from your partner.

If you want hardworking, honest and participative employees, then,

Be a hardworking, honest and participative employer.

And **be** more peaceful, kind, generous and forgiving if you want a more peaceful, kind, generous and forgiving world.

Be the person you want
others to be!

The best way
to teach
is to do.

Chapter **17**

Transition time

"Change is not achieved without inconvenience, even from worse to better."

Richard Hooker, 16th century

A huge reason why a lot of people keep returning to the PIT and don't get long term success is because they don't ride out the transition time — the period from the old behaviour to the new one that is forming.

They expect the transition to be easy and it's not. It's bloody challenging and PITMAN is there, all the way, coaxing, seducing, egging them back to their old ways, he says things like this:

"Go on have a puff on that cigarette — one puff won't hurt!"

"Go on lose your temper with your kids/staff/lover. They don't realise how hard you work!"

"Go on have an extra piece of chocolate cake, you deserve it!"

"Go on sleep in, you can go to the gym tomorrow!"

"Go on forget about finishing this job, you can do it later."

We have to pay attention to PITMAN and allow STICKMAN to take over. We constantly have to fight the urges to surrender to the 'easy' way.

You already know that the way to get out of a PITMAN frame of mind is to *DO* a behaviour that is opposite to what you are actually feeling or thinking.

If I'm feeling like an old cranky bum, I force myself to smile and be lovely to people. If I feel like quitting some work I'm doing because it's "too hard", I force myself to keep going. If I feel like stopping my run or weight session, I force myself to keep doing one lift after the next. If I feel like quitting anything, I force myself to keep dropping one foot in front of the next.

Deciding and doing are two very different routines. After the initial shock of separating from my husband, and adjusting to my new life, I found myself constantly looking for a potential partner. I would get on a plane and scan the cabin for any man I was attracted to. I would check his left hand. Wedding ring? *Next!*

I had spent the previous 18 years with someone in my life. I didn't know how to do single anymore. I kept searching everywhere I went.

With the wisdom of hindsight, I can see how in the first few months I was doing everything I could to avoid the transition time from being married to being single. Even though I chose to be single I would hate nights on the couch by myself.

And then one night when I was feeling particularly vulnerable, it hit me! I realised that I hadn't fully accepted that *I was on my own*. That was the night that I accepted that I was single!

There wasn't anyone to chat with me, hear me out, sit with me, hold and comfort me, not even anyone to fight with!

I started to cry ... and I cried and cried and cried. I was crying because I was scared about whether I could make it on my own. I was crying for what I had left behind and I was crying because I felt so empty and uncertain. I was crying for my little boys and their heart ache. This was one of the hardest periods of my life, but the only way out is through!

I sobbed my eyes out...*and then I surrendered.*

I surrendered to the realisation that I was on my own and I accepted that this transition would probably be uncomfortable. Gut-wrenchingly uncomfortable. I surrendered to the fact that I would feel lonely, yet this was a space I needed to get used to.

I now love time by myself (my time). I cherish it. I also realise that you don't need to be alone to feel lonely. Some of my most lonely moments have been within a relationship.

This alone time gave me the space to analyse my parenting, leadership and friendships. Over time I got to know myself, I got to explore the reasons why I think the way I do.

I gained the chance to evaluate the patterns that I had created in previous relationships and I discovered what I did to attract these types of people into my life.

During this period I worked out how I wanted to be treated and what I would and would not settle for. I worked out what is important to me, what I expect from future relationships and I defined areas where I will no longer compromise.

Did it happen overnight? No way! But it did happen. I remember one night, about five months after the separation; the tears came up once again after saying goodbye to my boys for another week as their father drove off with them.

This happened every week and each time I would cry so hard it felt as though my heart was being wrenched out of my chest: but that particular night I made the decision — I had cried enough.

There comes a time when we've grieved, cried and worried enough, after which it's time to move on. The lights go on and we wake up!

Of course I was still going to miss my boys dreadfully whenever I wasn't with them, but I was no longer going to allow my feelings to paralyse me.

I know that I will have many other times in my life where I will be touched by the events that will help transform who I am.

We all will.

And I know that I won't always handle them with STICKMAN fortitude.

The great thing now is that I decide when, where, with whom and for how long I go to my PIT!

I also know when I'm in there that it is no one else's fault.

Surrender,
and the lesson
will come.

Chapter **18**

Being right or choosing peace

As I get older I am finding that I am becoming more mellow in my responses to certain situations in life.

I now find myself letting things slide that I would have previously found incredibly irritating or upsetting. Wouldn't it have been great to have discovered that wisdom a little earlier in life so that I would not have wasted important energy on minor irritations and incidental issues?

As people mature I have often heard them say that they too have become more mellow (and I hope this characteristic isn't only restricted to those who are maturing). But maybe that is the rite of passage?

I am not saying you should be a pushover or a soft touch. I think respectful assertiveness coupled with a healthy self esteem are two of the most important traits anybody can possess.

A while back, I was on a long flight to London. (I am sure everyone who has been on a long flight can relate to this scenario). The woman sitting behind me kept banging my seat. It was a night flight and every time she bumped my seat she would wake me.

After about the eighth bump, I leaned around and said in a soft voice (which is not something that comes naturally to me at two o'clock in the morning), "Excuse me, you probably don't realise, but the back of my chair keeps getting bumped and I'm finding it hard to sleep. I was just wondering if you could be more aware of it, is that okay?"

We don't have any power over how another person responds or reacts. I would have loved to be able to report that she responded with "Oh, I'm so sorry, I didn't realize..." but alas, behind me sat Ms PITMAN!

"Well, I don't have that much room," she snapped.

I could have established that I was right but what was the point? An argument on a public aircraft would not have given me peace. I could have bought into it and got angry but I didn't. Gosh a few years back I would have!

I would have been a right Ms PITMAN and I would have probably said something really sarcastic like, "Lady, you've got the same amount of real estate as everybody else on the plane, funny how you're moving your little bot like you're at Jo's disco!"

Would I have felt better? Absolutely!

Well, maybe for a few seconds — but then she probably would have said something nastier then I would have had another go at her, then it would be my turn again, then hers and where would it stop? We would have both ended up so angry that neither of us would have been able to sleep.

I let it go and eventually she settled down.

When we're in our PITMAN state we feel that everyone else is against us. We see everything as a personal attack. "They did it to me!" Sometimes we get so stuck in having to win the fight, that we lose the war.

I remember hearing someone on the Oprah TV show say "What is more important, being right or having peace?" to which Oprah quickly replied with her famous humour "When everyone thinks I'm right, we'll all have peace". (Tongue in cheek of course!)

I think that statement makes such a valid point, how often does proving that we are right bring us peace?

It may give us some sense of satisfaction, but at what cost? It took me a long time to learn that powerful lesson.

I hope this is not simply me mellowing with time because it would be a shame to not get that pearl of absolute wisdom as young as possible.

What's more important: to be right or to have peace?

Sometimes we get so stuck in having to win the fight that we lose the war.

Chapter **19**

Your book
of life

I liken the entirety of my life to a great big book with its pages filled with all the experiences, people and adventures that have made up my life.

We all have our own *Book of Life* filled with our own stories and journeys. Some of our friends will be in our book for many chapters. Some may only feature in a few paragraphs while others will only appear for a few words.

Every encounter, discussion, facial expression, positive or nasty word to another human being goes into *their* Book of Life.

Now that you've read my book, I may feature in your Book of Life for a couple of words. But let me tell you, if I am going to be in someone's book, *I want to be* 84pt

"BOLD" not *10pt faded italic!* I want to make sure that I give everything I've got, as often as I can.

We all have an effect on each other. Every interaction with another human being helps that person write his or her book, as it helps us write our own. We're in metaphoric print forever.

The following story demonstrates the impact our influence has on another person's life. I can't say whether it's true or not but I am sure all of us can relate to the power of its message. I am reproducing it as I received it...

"Some time ago a mother punished her five year old daughter for wasting a roll of expensive gold wrapping paper.

Money was tight and she became even more upset when the child used the gold paper to decorate a box to put under the Christmas tree.

Nevertheless, the little girl brought the gift box to her mother the next morning and said, "This is for you, Mama".

The mother was embarrassed by her earlier overreaction, but her anger flared once more when she opened the box and found it was empty. She spoke to her daughter harshly.

"Don't you know young lady, when you give someone a present there's supposed to be something inside the package?"

The little girl had tears in her eyes as she replied, "Oh, Mama, it's not empty! I blew kisses into it until it was full."

The mother was crushed. She fell on her knees, put her arms around her little girl and begged her forgiveness for her thoughtless anger.

A short time later an accident took the life of this child. It is said that her mother kept that golden box by her bed all the years of her life.

Whenever she was discouraged or faced difficult problems she would open the box and take out an imaginary kiss and remember the love of the child who had put it there.

In a very real sense, each of us has been given a Golden Box filled with unconditional love and kisses from our children, family, friends and God. There is no more precious possession anyone could hold."

It still moves me to tears as I read this story. We all know times when we have said words that have crushed another person's spirit.

In contrast, there's the story of a boy who helped a fellow school mate pick up his books after he tripped over. Though virtual strangers, he decided to help out and they started to walk home together. They began a conversation which would be the first of many. Years later, the friend commented on how he had found it strange that his friend was taking all his school books home only to carry them back to school on Monday. His friend explained...

I took all my books home that day because I knew I wouldn't be returning to school. You see my friend, I was going home to kill myself. Then I dropped my books, you helped me and that changed everything!"

This beautiful story depicts the power of a kind deed and

how we sometimes never know how something we said or did changes another person's Book of Life. In this case, he added numerous more chapters to a book that would have been far too short!

So the next time you do or say anything, ask yourself, "How do I want to appear in this person's Book of Life?"

We are all
in metaphoric
print forever.

Chapter **20**

Cup filling

I t astonishes me how difficult it is for most of us to say something positive to another human being — unconditionally. So often we *think* wonderful things about others, and then keep the thoughts to ourselves instead of sharing them.

We all have emotional muscles — just as we have physical muscles. I call this The Emotional Muscle Factor™ or EMF for short. When exercised appropriately our EMF gives us amazing support when dealing with day-to-day life.

One of the most important emotional muscles we can possess is the ability to give people the kind of "FEEDBACK" that helps them feel better about themselves.

I call this 'cup filling' — which is where we fill somebody's emotional cup with comments and deeds that build their self esteem and self belief.

I was recently on a plane where I had the pleasure of being served by one of the happiest crews I had seen in a long time. As I was leaving, I was sufficiently impressed and wanted to say something complimentary.

Then PITMAN jumped into my head and said "Don't be silly, don't say anything, they'll think you're stupid."

Luckily STICKMAN yelled, "Walk your talk girl!" so as I left the plane, I placed my hand on one of the flight attendant's arms, smiled and said, "This is the happiest crew I have flown with in a long while."

She broke into open laughter, gave me a huge thank you and said, "You have no idea how much I needed to hear that!"

Her reaction was enough to show me that we *all* need our cup filled occasionally.

Check to see how readily you cup-fill. Do you find it easier to fill a stranger's cup than that of those you love? If so, is that because you tend to become over-critical of those you love? Have you stopped looking for the magic and do you only focus on the negatives?

In longer term relationships we tend to generalize the positives and specify the negatives.

We say, "I love you but…" as we go on to list all the things that annoy us about that person. In this way we become cup drillers and we weaken the very fabric that is needed for a strong relationship.

Making positive, uplifting comments takes some practice. It takes practice to notice the good in others and it takes practice to verbalise these observations.

I love to play a game with my kids called *Pass The Compliment*.

We sit in a circle and one of us begins by giving the person on the right two positive comments about why they love that person.

Once received this person can only respond with "thank you" and then they *pass it on* by giving the person on their right two positives — and so we work our way around our sacred hoop.

It works just as well when we return the other way so that we give and receive different compliments to and from each other.

This is a great game when travelling in the car because the trip gives us time to digest the compliment and so makes us think about why we love each other and why we are loved in return.

In doing so we are exercising our Emotional Muscle Factor™, and as we do our EMF grows with each expression of love.

There is nothing more rewarding than knowing your words have filled another person's cup.

Be a CUP FILLER not a CUP DRILLER and see the results, right there, on the faces of those you have touched!

In longer term relationships we
tend to generalize the positives
and specify the negatives.

Cup fillers
exercise their
Emotional
Muscles
Factor™.

Chapter **21**

Love letters

A s a parent, I regret to admit that I spend a lot of time nagging. 'Put your shoes away, feed the dog, clean your teeth, set the table, do your homework!'

I'm sure every parent can relate to this experience.

We can spend so much of our communication time being unconsciously negative which impinges on the time that may have been spent creating happy, loving memories for those whom we treasure.

What is it about the special people in your life that makes them so loveable? It is so important to remind the people that we love, why we love them.

To help restore the balance I write love letters. For example, I'll write a love letter every so often to my two beautiful boys.

I take some time out to tell them on paper what I think is wonderful, magnificent, precious, special, unique and fabulous about them!

An important rule when writing love letters is to never ever use the words 'but' or 'however' or mention anything that you're not happy with or that you feel that they could improve.

We pour it in at the top and then start drilling it out at the bottom. How often do we give (or get) a cup-fill only to end it with a cup drill?

We say all this "great, self esteem boosting" stuff and then completely destroy it by adding negative comments.

We often add comments that don't allow them to digest the positives, "You're doing so well at school *but*... if you spent less time on the PS2 you would do even better!"

I am not saying that we don't need to hear about the areas we need to work on. Of course we do. We just need to make sure that we *don't pollute the positives with negatives.*

Sometimes it's wonderful to bathe in the positives for a little while. It can also make it easier to take on board the "uglier" comments a little later.

Statistics show that on average 75% of communication in a relationship is negative whereas only 25% is positive.

It wasn't until I analysed these statistics that I realised how accurate they really were. Then it occurred to me.

If a person's cup is full, it probably won't be as difficult for that person to take criticism because the positive forms a healthy buffer. On the other hand, if a person's cup is empty, he or she is not going to be as receptive to constructive "FEEDBACK".

In fact, it will probably sting like hell.

So think about what you can do to remind the people in your life of what you love about them. How can you fill their cup?

Parents, write your sons and daughters the letter you have procrastinated about sending...for years!

We let stupid insecurities get in the way of helping others feel fantastic. Do you really think your baby (regardless of age) is going to be correcting your grammar or punctuation?

He or she will probably be so busy trying to read through misty eyes s/he wouldn't care if you wrote on toilet paper!

I remember one father who was more concerned about his handwriting being untidy than he was about filling his own sons' "cup to the brim".

My kids have kept every love letter I have given them.

So whether it's a Post-It Note with a short message popped into a lunch box, an email from the office to tell your daughter you were thinking of how much you love her, a funny card for your lover to say that after all these years he or she still turns your heart around, a quick text to say "I love you, son" or a five page essay detailing every scrumptious part of them that you love — do it!

Just do it!

I know it will be hard at first but it's like exercising any muscle that hasn't been given a regular workout. You may experience slight awkwardness at first but the more you work at it the easier it becomes, to the point where you just can't imagine life without writing letters that make other people feel great!

You never know, it may be your letter that reminds them

of how special they are when they think about doing something silly to themselves!

My mother and I had been close for many years. Unfortunately, through misconceptions, unrealistic expectations and not seeking the truth about each other we drifted apart to the point where hostility became part of our scarce communication.

The climax came one night when my mother and I had a massive phone-fight about the fallout from my marriage separation. There was a lot of screaming and yelling (more on my part) and lots of tears (from both of us). It was a huge show-down.

Everything I had never dared to say to her about my past came up as well as all the things that I had wanted from her but could never ask. It all came pouring out of my mouth with venom, anger and desperation.

I so badly wanted her to understand all that I had gone through. I wanted her to ease my pain — *feel my pain.*

For many years I had tried to convince myself that I didn't need my mother and that we weren't meant to have a close relationship. Now — feeling incredibly vulnerable — I wanted her to be a mummy and I wanted to be her little girl again.

But that night, something shifted. As she remained silent down her end of the line, I later realised that she was simply digesting the massive reality of my past that I had just sprung on her.

She had no idea what I had gone through because I had kept it from her so as not to hurt her. How ironic, by *not* sharing my truth with her we ended up hurting each other anyway!

When we conceal things from others, the unconscious mind picks it up but it can't decipher exactly what it is, it just knows that something isn't quite right.

People are not mind readers and when we conceal our truth from them, they have to make sense of the limited information we offer.

Their intuition may be screaming at them to pay attention — but we haven't given away enough information to validate their feelings.

That night all the pieces came together for my mother and me. We didn't magically create a new bond over night. It took lots of time, lots of talking, lots of patience and acceptance.

A few months after this eventful night I took a short trip to New Zealand and my mother babysat my boys. As I was leaving I noticed a yellow foolscap page lying on my bed. It was my mother's hand writing. I started to read. I tried to fight back the tears, my breath was taken away.

My mother had written me a love letter! Not just any old love letter. It was the most beautiful love letter in the world. She wrote it for me and in that moment as I blinked tears onto the page, I felt totally connected to her.

I felt her love and I knew she understood my past, which she knew she couldn't change, but just knowing that she was there for me, proud of me and loving me was everything that I needed.

That letter is now safely laminated and every time I read it I am reminded of my mother's love.

As I sat in Auckland Airport waiting pen in hand for my flight home, the words just flowed onto my page as I wrote back of my love for her.

To think we missed out on 10 years because we lost our way!

She celebrated her 80th birthday last week and I am so grateful we have found our way back to each other.

Some people say they don't have regrets. Well I do, I regret that I lost those 10 years through ignorance, pride and misunderstanding.

The only way out is through — yet we try to avoid the pain of confrontation by pretending we don't care.

Love letters work. I will keep writing those letters to my family and friends, and I hope you will write yours.

Jackson, 5

166

"People will forget what you said and they may forget what you did, but they will never, ever forget how you made them feel!"

Unknown

Statistics show that on average 75% of communication in a relationship is negative whereas only 25% is positive.

Chapter **22**

Your past cannot hurt you

Often the reason we don't move forward is because we can spend thirty years getting over something that happened to us for five minutes when we were four!!

I am not being frivolous here. I know from firsthand experience the potential destructiveness of a painful childhood — but you know what I know more? I know the absolute destructiveness of letting our past destroy our today and our tomorrows.

Here is a fact that we briefly touched on in the first chapter. Your past cannot hurt you. *Your past does not hurt you.*

It is the *meaning* you place on your past that hurts you. Change the meaning and you will change how you respond to that memory. There will be a biological response in the brain to this new meaning.

Will it happen instantly? No! We know by now that habits, even bad thinking habits, take time to re-wire.

It's all about interpretation. Some experiences from our past give us a surge of energy. The problem is we get attached to the charge that comes from the interpretation of this event. From this we derive routines that beg attention, even sympathy.

During a management workshop I recall a participant sharing this story. "A girl used to wet her pants at school," she started. "She would try to cover it up by saying that her parents would beat her — but we all knew she was lying."

I asked how the participant knew the child was lying and she said that she couldn't see how wetting her pants could relate to her parents smacking her.

So I shared a story from my past. "When my father was angry he had very little self control. If we had done something wrong, he would beat us quite badly. Whenever he called my name in *that tone* or when he started to beat me, I too would lose bladder control. So maybe she wasn't lying. Maybe she was just looking for help."

A fabulous discussion about "interpretation" followed.

As I was driving home that evening I allowed my thoughts to wander back to that memory. I thought about me as a little girl and how awful it was to have so much fear that I sometimes lost bladder control. Embarrassing, isn't it?

As the road stretched before me I started to feel sad, angry and helpless. I was immersed in feelings I had felt a thousand times before. Even though I hadn't brought back this particular memory for a long time, here I was practically in tears.

Where was I?

In the PIT!

I shook my head, gave myself a good talking to, then questioned myself quite logically: "Have you derived all the learnings that you needed to get from this experience? Yes. Do you need to learn anything more from this? No. Are you sure? Yes. Then get over it! I think you have milked this one for everything you can, Terry."

So I changed the meaning of wetting my pants!

That experience taught me humility. It also revealed the false power an adult has over a child. I was able to gain some understanding because my father had come from a similar background and I was simply a victim of a victim.

I learned to forgive and to develop compassion. I learned to stop wishing that it had never happened.

I learned so much from my upbringing. Yes I *had* moved on, yet in that reflective moment in the car, (with a little bit of self pity and self indulgence) I had allowed myself to go straight back into the PIT.

When we have a painful memory we sometimes choose to hang onto the pain associated with it because it stirs us and sets the adrenal gland racing which is highly addictive. But there comes a time when you have to say "enough"!

As I mentioned before, I am not condoning the behaviour but I am accepting that it happened and there was a lot to learn from it.

How unfortunate that we sometimes waste valuable learning opportunities simply because we are stuck in the negative emotions of past experiences.

Another way to separate yourself from your emotions is to check that you are being dissociated as you recall the memory. Are you looking at it as though it is a movie in which you are watching yourself? To what extent are you emotionally involved in the replay?

Ask yourself these questions and in this way you will disconnect yourself from the emotions involved which will make it easier for you to change the meaning of whatever happened and gain wisdom from the experience.

I now look back on my past events and I wouldn't change a thing about them. Would it have been good to learn the same lessons in a different, less painful way? Absolutely! But hey, it didn't happen that way so I'll find the learnings any way I know how.

We will never see the powerful insights we have gained from our life experiences if we are drowning in the misery, pity and sorrow of the PIT. It really is a dark place so why stay there?

The wisdom and peace we're seeking happens outside the PIT.

It is not your past that hurts you.

It is the meaning you place on your past that hurts you. Change the meaning and set yourself free.

Your past does not
hurt you.

It is the meaning you
place on your past
that hurts you.

Change the meaning
and you will change
how you respond to
that memory.

Chapter **23**

Play at 100%.
Be here
and make a
difference

As you know, one of my favorite sayings is:
There are two times in life... now & too late!
I love it because it is so true.

The only time we have is this moment right now and what we do with it. The moment you had five minutes ago is gone forever! That's how life works.

How we act in each moment is up to us. Giving 100 per cent means giving it everything you have. I'm not talking about running around like Odie the dog and falling into bed each night exhausted.

It's about playing at 100 per cent in all that you do — whether it's kicking a ball with your kids, working on a business document, riding a bike in the park or having an afternoon nap — it's about doing it all to your best ability: being *in the moment*. It is also about being passionate.

My father taught me about passion and giving 100 per cent. I landed my first job at age 15 scrubbing cupboards in a cafeteria. Not my idea of a great vocation!

My father was dying of cancer at the time and one day, before I left home to catch the bus for my ordeal, he called me into his bedroom.

As he lay in bed, he said, "Go scrub those cupboards girl, like there's no tomorrow." We were doing it tough and the money would come in handy. "But Dad…" I whined, "I don't want a job scrubbing greasy cupboards!"

"It's good money, so go and do the job" he said.

After our conversation I remember travelling on the bus with a completely different perception. I was no longer scrubbing cupboards, I was saving my family!! I scrubbed those cupboards so hard I almost brought the wood-grain back up!

I finished the day with greasy hair, greasy skin and my boss admiring my hard work. Well let me tell you, within three weeks I was the milkshake maker. Straight up that corporate ladder!

What my father was really telling me was the old adage that Stephen Covey the author of *The Seven Habits of Highly*

Effective People has made famous "The enemy of your best is your good".

When I heard those words my first reaction was "HUGGH!" I had to play that message over and over in my head until it clicked with me.

The enemy of your best is when you choose good.

How are the kids? Good.

How's work? Good.

How have you been? Good.

It's as if we accept 'good' as our standard, not our best! Can you imagine what might happen if we aimed for best, instead of good, every time? We could quite possibly have the most wonderful life imaginable!

But why don't we? We get too comfortable doing what we know, aiming for things we are certain can be easily achieved. We do them at a level that no longer presents a challenge for us and avoids the possibility of stress. But it is these challenges and levels of uncertainty that keep us young. The complexity boosts our system, keeps our hearts and minds ticking and slows down that aging process.

It is no coincidence that some people retire to a way of pure relaxation often have plummeting health issues. The body simply shuts down and terminates the areas that are not in use.

So I invite you the next time you are walking along the beach or the park with the people or person you have chosen to spend your life with, walk along that beach or park as if you will never ever walk along that beach or park with them ever again.

We tend to complain about our lives but what if we considered the alternatives? What if you didn't have what you have? I can't imagine my life with those two little beds empty.

And the next time you're holding a baby in your arms, hold that baby like you'll never hold another baby again.

It may seem a strange thing to say especially if you don't have your own children but I'm suggesting you hold that baby tenderly for the memory of a 14 month old son of an old friend.

He was only 14 months old when his little life ended. He was accidentally run over in the driveway of their house.

I used to bounce my babies in my arms to put them asleep (I think there is something special about falling asleep in your mother's arms). Some nights my arm would hurt from the weight, so I would just bounce them faster! When I got really frustrated I would feel angry and think, "Just go to sleep will you".

In those moments I would think of that 14 month old boy and say to myself, "Hurt away, it doesn't matter, I have my baby in my arms."

So the next time you're spending time with someone you care about, treat that person as if this is their last day on earth and you are one of the last people to have a positive influence on their life. Reach deep inside yourself and find what you need to say or do to make people feel right.

We spend so much time focusing on ourselves that we forget how powerful we can be in the life of another.

Lao Tzu, the author of the *Tao Te Ching,* wrote, "There is no more noble job on earth than to be of service to another human being!"

The enemy
of our best
is our
good!

Chapter **24**

The truth

You know the feeling when someone tells you a story that you sense isn't true? After a while you begin to suspect something about the story and the more you listen, the more your skin starts to crawl until you begin to shuffle uneasily in your seat.

There is a part of you that knows it just isn't true because it doesn't feel right.

And then you listen to someone else's story that resonates with every part of your being and you know that every word is true. Although you may not have even heard the concepts before, there is something within you that recognises that the message comes from a place of absolute honesty.

Sometimes I'll read or hear something and even though I have never heard it before, something inside tells me it's absolutely true. That feeling is our innate truth — it's that part of us that allows us to separate the crap from the real stuff.

We all have this ability to sense what is real and what isn't. If we pay attention hard enough, these truths will come to us from anywhere and anyone.

Maybe something stirred in you as you read this book. I hope that you paid attention.

Sometimes it is hard for us to "hear the truth within" because, regardless of how negative this state may be, we may be so stuck in a certain behaviour that we are not yet willing to move on.

I know of *some* people who keep themselves ill (unconsciously but also sometimes consciously) because of the 'benefits' they get from being ill. It might be attention, excuses, less pressure or dependency — whatever 'benefit' they get overrides the freedom of living their life in truth.

"It's not my fault!" they cry as they continue to not *do* anything that will contribute to their getting better.

It's just the same when we blame others for the way we react. Our anger, sarcasm, aloofness, self pity all become someone else's fault. "If they hadn't behaved that way I wouldn't have reacted this way!" is the cry of the person who denies the truth of their own lack of self control.

We all can run from truth at times. It can be overwhelming to take total personal responsibility for ourselves but at the end of the day it is only our truth that will set us on the right path.

So listen, PAY ATTENTION in those moments when it hurts to hear the truth about yourself.

Ask "What do I need to learn from this?"

"What am I suppose to be getting here?"

STICKMAN will help you to find an answer.

It may not happen immediately and may not be easy but if you are serious about "getting the truth" then you will find it because the truth will set you free.

The truth will set you free.

– John 8:31.

Chapter **25**

The buck stops with me!

Be conscious of your state

*B*e conscious of your state

One of the easiest ways to tell if you're in a PITMAN state or not, is to check where you are laying blame. When we're in the PIT we tend to blame everyone and everything for how we feel or what is or isn't happening in our life.

Take personal responsibility

STICKMAN is about taking personal responsibility for how we perceive the situations and events in our life. "The buck stops with us!"

It is no-one else's job to make us feel happy, satisfied or

loved. It is our responsibility. Taking personal responsibility means that you are in charge of your life.

I think there is no greater travesty in this life than to have not become the person you were meant to become.

Change the meaning

As I said earlier we all have "stuff" that happens to us. It would be great to be able to learn our lessons a different way, an easier way, but for some of us those lessons were and continue to be painful.

Where do we think wisdom comes from? You don't get wisdom without a few spoonfuls of grief gravy.

Remember, it is never our past that hurts us. It is the meaning we place on our past that hurts us. If we change the meaning, we change our perception and feelings that we have about the situation or person.

We can spend our lives in blame but you will not gain anything this way. I don't condone people's inappropriate behaviour, I do believe though that most people are doing the best they can with what they know at the time. If they knew better they probably would have done better.

Lick your wounds, find the wisdom in the pain and use this to go forth and live the adventure called YOUR LIFE.

Commitment

We began this journey with Johann Wolfgang Goethe, BEGIN IT NOW! How appropriate to now end with it. I find one of the most common traits among successful people is commitment.

Commitment is being willing to do whatever it takes to get the job done — regardless of the job! It could be mowing the lawn, going to your child's concert, running a company with integrity, being honest, being fit and healthy... it doesn't really matter what the goal is as long as we have commitment, we will achieve.

Commitment in a relationship is often a funny thing. Most of us would say that we are committed to our partner and kids, to our employer or staff, to our friends. But usually when push comes to shove, most people in a relationship will threaten each other with the relationship when things get a bit tough.

Isn't it true! We may say these things in jest but remember the unconscious mind believes everything we say.

"Go on then, pack your bags. I'm not stopping you." "I've had it with this relationship... I'm out of here!" "They wouldn't know what hit them if I left this place!"

When we make comments like that we put chinks in our relationship armour. No wonder so many of us are walking around feeling battered!

People wonder why the magic leaves their relationship, yet if they were really committed to it they would listen for the languaging they use when communicating with their partner.

Sarcasm, nasty little jibes, criticism and judgement all serve to decay the very foundation you have been trying to build.

There are two times in life... now & too late!

- Do something, take action.

- Use STICKMAN as your support mechanism, always being aware of the seductiveness of PITMAN.

- Decide that you will start to make a difference in your life and the lives of those around you, today.

- Life is so precious and each and every one of us has many gifts. For some, these gifts are buried in the heaviness of the PIT, but they are there. KEEP DIGGING!

- Have the courage to go find them and know that your place in life is a vital one — if you don't know your life's purpose, relax, you're probably doing it anyway!

And finally,

remember that courage only comes *after* you face the fear, so face your fears head on and meet that wonderful, magnificent person...

called you!

Do something, take action, begin it now!

Dedication

I dedicate this book to the beautiful Lynn and thank her for touching my life in ways that are beyond expression. I share the following with you as a gift from Lynn to us all. May her soul be sprinkled throughout all of our lives.

The Present

In a university commencement address several years ago, Brian Dyson, the CEO of Coca Cola Enterprises, spoke of the relation of work to one's other commitments.

"Imagine life as a game in which you are juggling five balls in the air. The names of these five balls are: work, family, health, friends and spirit.

You are very busy keeping all of these balls in the air.

You will soon understand that work is a rubber ball. If you drop it, it will bounce back. The other four balls, family, health, friends and spirit are made of glass.

What will happen if you drop one of these balls?

They will be irrevocably scuffed, marked, nicked, damaged or even shattered. They will never be the same again.

It is very important to understand this and strive for balance in our lives.

So how do we keep the balance in our life?

Let us learn to value ourselves and refrain from comparing

ourselves with others. It is *because* we are different that each of us is so special.

Let us set our own goals. Only we know what is best for ourselves.

Nourish and cherish the people and things closest to our hearts. Let us cling to them as we would life, for without them life is meaningless.

Let us learn to live in the present moment and learn from the past and plan for the future. By living our lives one day at a time we live **all** the days of our life.

Let us contribute, while we still have something to give. Nothing is over until we stop trying.

Let us not be afraid to admit that we are less than perfect. It is this fragile thread that binds us to each other.

Let us not be afraid to encounter risks. It is by taking chances that we learn how to be brave.

Love is all around us. The more we are aware of love the more we find.

The quickest way to receive love is to give love.

The fastest way to lose love is to hold it too tightly.

The best way to keep love is to give it wings.

Let us remember not to run through life so fast that we forget not only where we have been, but also where we are going.

Remember that a person's greatest emotional need is to be appreciated.

Let us continue to learn. Knowledge is weightless, a treasure we can always carry easily.

Neither time nor words can be retrieved. Let us learn to use both wisely.

Life is a journey, not a race. It should be savoured each step of the way.

Yesterday is history and tomorrow is a mystery. Today is a gift and that is why we call it...

The Present.

Let us contribute,
while we still have
something to give.
Nothing is over until
we stop trying.

WELL DONE!

Where did STICKMAN® and PITMAN come from?

I am often asked "How did you come up with these two characters?"

STICKMAN® and PITMAN evolved over a 15 year period during my years as a business/people skills trainer. Stickman gets his name because I would draw a stick figure on the flipchart (see below) to explain the Mind Language® process. I wasn't sure what to call him so I just said Stickman while I was trying to figure out a good name.

Then one day, while I was presenting the Pit of Misery and talking about Pit parties, Pit Posture, Pit Prattle etc, someone in the audience called out "sounds like a PITMAN to me and hey presto! There it was ... PITMAN and all of a sudden STICKMAN® sounded perfect as well!

I have added to the terminologies as time has gone on so now we have Stickchicks, Stickgirls, Stickboys, Pitboys, Pitgirls etc. That's the magic of these two wonderful characters, they just keep growing and evolving.

STICKMAN® is a registered trademark of Terry Hawkins.

Tell us your stories!

TM

*A*s you can see *There Are Two Times in Life … NOW & TOO LATE!* is sprinkled with stories of heroes who have been impacted by STICKMAN in the moment. I would love to hear your personal stories.

Email them to Terry at
mail@peopleinprogress.com.au

Terry Hawkins

Trainer – speaker – author

F ive minutes with Terry Hawkins and you will be inspired, there's no escaping it. This lady is a dynamo, a powerhouse oozing fun, laughter and emotion with every breath. Today she is regarded as one of the most successful and sought-after speakers in Australia, New Zealand and increasingly, across the globe, for her dynamic presentations and innovative training programs which have already affected more than 100,000 employees from companies like Mecca Cosmetics, Ray White Real Estate, Kookai and Readymix Rinker.

Terry grew up in an average home in suburban Brisbane. At the age of 15, her father died and the teenager was forced into a parental role for her siblings. She held multiple jobs after finishing school – few offering little career hope – until she became a salesperson with Just Jeans. Determined to succeed despite having no retail experience – she didn't tell them that of course – Terry treated her customers as friends and her sales went through the roof.

Soon she was manager and quadrupled sales, before Terry got to work to transform the company's staff training manuals. Her quest was to revolutionise staff training and she did. After Just Jeans, Terry continued to climb the corporate ladder and soon had a reputation for her amazing ability to engage and train staff, landing her a national training position.

After life threw her some interesting circumstances, Terry took the plunge and opened her own training company – People In Progress – at the age of 27. It started with a card table and a beloved typewriter, which she tapped away at with two fingers. "I didn't care about my plush office, or lack thereof. I just wanted to help people. I knew I could help people and make a difference," Terry said.

Like everything she does, Terry jumped into the business 100 per cent. It wasn't without its obstacles and setbacks, which Terry describes as "difficult" at times, but says the only option is to "walk through it". She "forged" ahead despite rejections and today laughs about her first "yes" to training, which sent her into a frenzy to write the course. "I said I could only do half day seminars, because that was all I could fit in, but really, I needed the other half of the day to actual write the manual!!". Today Terry leads the way as a pioneer in innovative and inspiring learning.

When not on the road, Terry lives on the Northern Beaches NSW with her two beautiful sons Harison and Jackson. She is a Certified Master Practitioner of NLP, Time Line Therapy and Hypnotherapy.

Rather than bamboozle the audience with jargon, Terry's aim is to interact with people in a way that is nothing short of spectacular. She's funny, engaging, insightful and inspiring. It's hard to convey on paper just how lasting her impact on you will be. She is one of those rare people who will touch your head and your heart and you'll remember it forever.

People In Progress –
a company on a mission

P eople In Progress has a simple mandate – to make a
powerful, positive impact on the human condition.
And we're doing it!

We are educators – we assist others to be all that they
can be by. We are an example of all that we train, using our
own methodologies as our guide. We create abundance – for
ourselves and those we represent in all main arenas of life.

People In Progress was established by Terry Hawkins in
1988, and today is recognised as one of the most respected,
innovative and results-based training companies in Australia.
Every program and system is unique and tailor-made for each
client, based on Terry's successful career in corporate and
business training, and coupled with her amazing approach
to life.

People In Progress offers powerful training, industry
benchmarks and effective support systems for any business
or organisation in an exciting, fun and inspiring way. You
will be blown away by Terry's dedication to improving your
company or organisations from a woman who simply wants
people to "love learning".

As thousands and thousands have said before …
you won't believe it till you've tried it!

For more information on People In Progress, visit
www.peopleinprogress.com.au

STICKMAN® Rules!

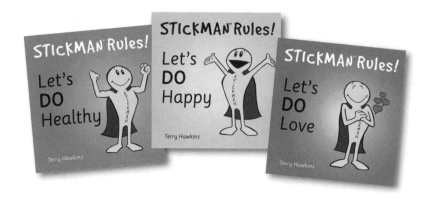

Y ears 7 to 14 are the most formative years of a child's life.

This is our chance to help our kids have a belief system to make personal choices about life regardless of their environment.

The STICKMAN® Rules! series is a simple, down-to-earth string of beautifully designed books that will give your kids a support mechanism.

Help them discover the support and brilliance of STICKMAN® and the dangers and sadness associated with PITMAN through this incredible series by Terry Hawkins.

For more information or to purchase a copy, visit
www.peopleinprogress.com.au